ISBN: 978-0-7710-5748-9

Library and Archives Canada Cataloguing in Publication is available upon request

Published simultaneously in the United States of America by McClelland & Stewart, a division of Penguin Random House LLC, a Penguin Random House Company

Library of Congress Control Number is available upon request

Printed and bound in the United States of America

McClelland & Stewart,
a division of Penguin Random House Canada Limited,
a Penguin Random House Company
www.penguinrandomhouse.ca

1   2   3   4   5   21   20   19   18   17

McClelland & Stewart

CONTENTS

INTRODUCTION
FOR THE VERY FIRST TIME

Since their inception in 1962, the Houston Astros have been without a World Series title to their name. This year, however, everything changed.

The Astros won their first world championship thanks to superstar sluggers such as Jose Altuve, Carlos Correa and George Springer. But that wasn't all; the team could not have gotten as far it did without clutch pitching by Justin Verlander, Dallas Keuchel and Lance McCullers Jr. For most of the season, Houston had the best record in the American League.

Verlander joined the team in September and showed why he's a former Cy Young Award winner with his dominant repertoire, and carried the team through the ALCS, where he won MVP honors. Leadoff man Springer had a breakout season, leading the team in home runs and garnering his first All-Star nomination. Rookie Yuli Gurriel was consistent all season batting in the middle of the order. And, of course, perennial MVP candidate Jose Altuve was one of the best all-around players in the Big Leagues.

Houston outplayed Boston in the ALDS, winning in four games, and then faced off against the Yankees in the ALCS. Home-field advantage was key, as the Astros remained undefeated at Minute Maid Park through the first two rounds of the playoffs. Finally, as they reached only their second Fall Classic in franchise history, the Astros fought tooth and nail against the power-laden Dodgers, prevailing in seven games and earning the club's first-ever World Series title.

IN JUST HIS THIRD SEASON AT THE HELM, ASTROS MANAGER A.J. HINCH (BOTTOM) LED THE TEAM TO A WORLD SERIES TITLE IN AN EPIC SEVEN-GAME BATTLE AGAINST THE DODGERS. THE VICTORY LIFTED THE HOUSTON COMMUNITY AFTER THE TRAGEDY AND DEVASTATION OF HURRICANE HARVEY OVER THE SUMMER.

THANKS TO THE CLUTCH HITTING OF
RISING STARS SUCH AS ALEX BREGMAN
(TOP) AND CARLOS CORREA (LEFT), THE
ASTROS GAVE THEIR FANS SOMETHING
TO CHEER FOR ALL SUMMER LONG,
WINNING 101 REGULAR-SEASON GAMES
AND POWERING THEIR WAY TO A WORLD
SERIES TITLE IN THEIR FIRST FALL CLASSIC
APPEARANCE SINCE 2005.

THE 2017 ASTROS ACCOMPLISHED SOMETHING THAT HALL OF FAMERS JEFF BAGWELL AND CRAIG BIGGIO, PICTURED HERE ON A MURAL INSIDE MINUTE MAID PARK, COULDN'T: CAPTURE THE FRANCHISE'S FIRST-EVER WORLD SERIES TITLE. THE TEAM'S FEROCIOUS COMBINATION OF CARLOS CORREA AND JOSE ALTUVE (OPPOSITE) BECAME ONE OF THE MOST FEARED SHORTSTOP-SECOND BASE DUOS IN ALL OF BASEBALL.

EVERYTHING'S BIGGER IN TEXAS, FROM THE CROWDS AT MINUTE MAID PARK DURING THE FALL CLASSIC, TO THE CARGO THAT THE TRAIN CONDUCTOR CARRIES BEYOND THE OUTFIELD WALL (BELOW), TO THE KINDS OF CELEBRITIES THAT CHEER FOR THE WORLD SERIES CHAMPIONS, INCLUDING FORMER PRESIDENT GEORGE W. BUSH (LEFT).

MARWIN GONZALEZ (ABOVE) EMERGED AS A KEY PIECE OF THE ASTROS PUZZLE IN 2017, HITTING OVER .300 AND BLASTING MORE THAN 20 HOME RUNS WHILE PLAYING MULTIPLE POSITIONS FOR THE FALL CLASSIC CHAMPIONS.

ALEX BREGMAN (TOP) CAME UP CLUTCH IN THE WORLD SERIES FOR HOUSTON, SCORING TWO RUNS AND DRIVING IN THE GAME-WINNING TALLY WITH A WALK-OFF SINGLE IN GAME 5. JUSTIN VERLANDER WAS NAMED ALCS MVP FOR HIS STELLAR OUTINGS AGAINST THE YANKEES, AND POSTED A 2.21 ERA IN SIX POSTSEASON APPEARANCES THIS SEASON.

THE ASTROS ARE IN POSITION TO CONTEND FOR THE WORLD SERIES TITLE FOR YEARS TO COME WITH A YOUNG CORE OF SLUGGERS SUCH AS GEORGE SPRINGER AND CARLOS CORREA. SPRINGER SLUGGED FIVE FALL CLASSIC HOMERS, WHILE CORREA DROVE IN 14 RUNS IN 18 PLAYOFF GAMES THIS YEAR.

WORLD SERIES

GAME 1, OCTOBER 24
LOS ANGELES 3, HOUSTON 1

	1	2	3	4	5	6	7	8	9	R	H	E
HOUSTON	0	0	0	1	0	0	0	0	0	1	3	0
LOS ANGELES	1	0	0	0	0	2	0	0	x	3	6	0

WP: KERSHAW LP: KEUCHEL SV: JANSEN
HR: HOU: BREGMAN LAD: TAYLOR, TURNER

Pitching just like the legend sitting in the second row at Dodger Stadium, Sandy Koufax, left-hander Clayton Kershaw overwhelmed the explosive Astros with 11 strikeouts in seven dazzling innings, and Justin Turner slugged a tiebreaking two-run homer off Dallas Keuchel for a 3-1 Dodgers win in the opener of the World Series.

The two-hour, 28-minute game — the quickest in Fall Classic history since Game 4 of the 1992 Series (2:21) — gave the Dodgers a 1-0 lead in the Series.

Turner's sixth-inning home run — hit using a lighter bat than in his first two plate appearances — followed a two-out walk to Chris Taylor, who opened the bottom of the first by launching Keuchel's first pitch 447 feet for his third postseason homer.

"I think CT is the hero," Turner said of his NLCS co-MVP. "He got us on the board early. He drew the two-out walk, stayed in the zone and gave me the opportunity. That's what he's been doing for us all year long. He's the spark plug at the top of the lineup, and when he goes, we go."

Before the game, someone had scrawled a plan on the whiteboard in Los Angeles' clubhouse. "Hit these boys in their mouths & don't look back!" the message read. The Dodgers did just that.

"Taylor hit a first-pitch four-seamer out of the yard, kind of hit us in the jaw," Keuchel said.

"He's that guy you want up there in the big moments," Dodgers Manager Dave Roberts said of Turner. "He doesn't scare off."

Los Angeles' first World Series appearance in 29 years began with the temperature reaching a record 103 degrees at first pitch, but the heat didn't bother Kershaw, who in his World Series debut allowed only three hits and a run on Alex Bregman's homer leading off the fourth.

"[For] the first time in a while, we've seen all three of his pitches synced up," said Roberts. "He just was repeating the delivery, held the velocity. Was throwing the baseball where he needed to, where he wanted to."

Kershaw, in a franchise-record-setting seventh postseason victory, didn't walk a batter, and his 11 K's tied for the most by a Dodgers player in a World Series game since Koufax's 15 in Game 1 in 1963 against the Yankees. They also were the most for any pitcher in the World Series since the Yanks' Orlando Hernandez had 12 in 2000, and the most strikeouts by any one pitcher against the Astros this year. The only other pitcher with 11 strikeouts and no walks in a World Series game was current Dodgers executive Don Newcombe (1949).

Brandon Morrow pitched the eighth inning and Kenley Jansen the ninth for the save. Kershaw said he told Roberts he had another inning in him after throwing only 83 pitches, but the manager went to this October's best bullpen.

"You know with our bullpen, it doesn't matter," Kershaw said. "So I told him I was good to go, but how can you argue with what [Morrow] and Kenley are doing back there? They proved it once again. This is a really good hitting team, [so] there's little room for error."

The Astros fell to 1-5 on the road this postseason, compared with 6-0 at Minute Maid Park.

"Sometimes you have to tip the hat to the other team," Houston second baseman Jose Altuve said. "You have to tip your hat to Clayton. It was really tough to hit him. He did a really good job."

IN THE FIRST FALL CLASSIC MATCHUP AT DODGER STADIUM IN NEARLY THREE DECADES, HOUSTON SKIPPER A.J. HINCH (CENTER) OPTED TO START KEUCHEL IN THE SERIES OPENER. THE ACE THREW 6.2 SOLID INNINGS FOR THE ASTROS, BUT TOOK A TOUGH LOSS AS KERSHAW STYMIED THE HOUSTON OFFENSE OVER SEVEN SPECTACULAR INNINGS. THE GAME WAS THE QUICKEST WORLD SERIES TILT IN 25 YEARS, FINISHED IN TWO HOURS AND 28 MINUTES.

"Keuchel was really good tonight. He was just a pitch or two less than Kershaw. He wasn't as fancy with the punch-outs. But take nothing away from these guys, it was a well-pitched game on both sides."

ASTROS MANAGER A.J. HINCH

AFTER SURRENDERING A LEADOFF HOME RUN TO TAYLOR, KEUCHEL (FAR LEFT) SETTLED DOWN AND LASTED INTO THE SEVENTH INNING. BREGMAN (TOP) PROVIDED RUN SUPPORT FOR HIS ACE WITH A SOLO SHOT, BUT TURNER ANSWERED BACK WITH A HOMER OF HIS OWN IN THE SIXTH INNING.

WORLD SERIES CHAMPIONS 2017

WORLD SERIES

GAME 2, OCTOBER 25
HOUSTON 7, LOS ANGELES 6

	1	2	3	4	5	6	7	8	9	10	11	R	H	E
HOUSTON	0	0	1	0	0	0	0	1	1	2	2	7	14	1
LOS ANGELES	0	0	0	0	1	2	0	0	0	2	1	6	5	0

WP: DEVENSKI LP: McCARTHY
HR: HOU: GONZALEZ, ALTUVE, CORREA, SPRINGER
LAD: PEDERSON, SEAGER, PUIG, CULBERSON

The Astros found themselves with no shortage of heroic moments and performances in Game 2 of the World Series.

Three outs from a daunting deficit in the Fall Classic, the Astros pulled off two improbable rallies against Los Angeles' vaunted bullpen and shocked a Dodger Stadium crowd with an 11-inning victory to even the Series at one game apiece.

The back-and-forth thriller featured eight homers, including five extra-inning home runs.

"That's an incredible game on so many levels, so many ranges of emotion," Astros Manager A.J. Hinch said. "If you like October baseball, if you like any kind of baseball, that's one of the most incredible games you'll ever be a part of."

When Chris Devenski got Yasiel Puig to swing through a 3-2 change-up for the final out, Houston breathed a huge sigh of relief and earned the first World Series victory in club history.

Marwin Gonzalez led off the top of the ninth with a game-tying home run off Kenley Jansen, one of the premier closers in the game. Jose Altuve and Carlos Correa led off the 10th with homers off former teammate Josh Fields, putting Houston ahead, 5-3, to become the first pair to hit extra-inning back-to-back blasts in the World Series.

The Dodgers extended the game in the bottom of the 10th with some clutch hitting. Puig homered to lead off against Astros closer Ken Giles. After Yasmani Grandal and Austin Barnes struck out, Logan Forsythe walked, took second on a wild pitch and was singled home by NLCS hero Enrique Hernandez, barely beating Josh Reddick's throw to tie the game at 5.

Springer hit a two-run shot in the 11th off Brandon McCarthy, who was L.A.'s eighth reliever in the game.

Charlie Culberson, inserted into Cody Bellinger's cleanup spot in a double-switch, homered with two outs in the bottom of the 11th to bring up Puig again, but Devenski struck him out to seal the improbable victory.

"I have to tell you, this is one of the craziest games I've ever played," Altuve said. "I really thank God for the opportunity to be here."

Houston third baseman Alex Bregman agreed. "It's gotta be the greatest game I've ever played in and probably everybody in here."

Gonzalez's homer in the ninth came on an 0-2 cutter, signaling the first blown save for Jansen after successfully converting the first 12 of his postseason career, an MLB record.

An inning earlier, the Astros cut the lead to 3-2 with a leadoff double by Bregman off Brandon Morrow and a one-out single up the middle by Correa off Jansen, snapping the Dodgers bullpen's scoreless-innings streak at 28. Houston took the first lead of the game in the third by parlaying three singles off starter Rich Hill, who was removed after four innings.

Los Angeles scored in the fifth inning on a two-out homer by Joc Pederson, his first longball since July 26, ending starter Justin Verlander's no-hit bid. An inning later, Corey Seager followed a two-out walk to Chris Taylor with an opposite-field two-run home run to give the Dodgers a 3-1 lead.

When the four-hour, 19-minute epic was finally over, Hinch was in no mood to be satisfied with the Astros' first World Series victory.

"I think the fourth one," he said, "that will be the one to bring home to the city."

IN GAME 2 OF THE WORLD SERIES, GONZALEZ (ABOVE) WAS REWARDED WITH A SHOWER OF SUNFLOWER SEEDS AFTER HE HELPED THE ASTROS SLUG THEIR WAY TO THE CLUB'S FIRST FALL CLASSIC WIN IN FRANCHISE HISTORY. HIS LEADOFF HOMER IN THE NINTH INNING TIED THE GAME AND CAPPED A COMEBACK THAT STARTED WITH BREGMAN'S (TOP) DOUBLE IN THE EIGHTH INNING. PRIOR TO THE GAME, COUNTRY STAR BRAD PAISLEY (OPPOSITE) SANG THE NATIONAL ANTHEM AND JOSE ALTUVE RECEIVED THE HANK AARON AWARD FROM COMMISSIONER ROB MANFRED AND AARON HIMSELF.

"That's an incredible game on so many levels, so many ranges of emotion. If you like October baseball, if you like any kind of baseball, that's one of the most incredible games you'll ever be a part of."

ASTROS MANAGER A.J. HINCH

ALTUVE AND CORREA (OPPOSITE) BECAME THE FIRST PAIR OF TEAMMATES IN WORLD SERIES HISTORY TO HIT BACK-TO-BACK HOMERS IN EXTRA INNINGS. THEIR HEROICS SET UP SPRINGER'S DRAMATIC BLAST OFF BRANDON McCARTHY THAT SENT THE FALL CLASSIC TO HOUSTON KNOTTED AT ONE GAME APIECE.

WORLD SERIES

GAME 3, OCTOBER 27
HOUSTON 5, LOS ANGELES 3

	1	2	3	4	5	6	7	8	9	R	H	E
LOS ANGELES	0	0	1	0	0	2	0	0	0	3	4	2
HOUSTON	0	4	0	0	1	0	0	0	x	5	12	0

WP: McCULLERS JR. LP: DARVISH SV: PEACOCK
HR: HOU: GURRIEL

McCULLERS JR. (ABOVE) HELPED FIRE UP THE HOME CROWD AND PICKED UP THE
WIN IN GAME 3. THE FANS AT MINUTE MAID PARK HAD YET ANOTHER OPPORTUNITY
TO SCREAM ITS "M-V-P!" CHANT FOR JOSE ALTUVE, AS THE SUPERSTAR DOUBLED
DURING THE ASTROS' FOUR-RUN SECOND INNING.

The Astros got to Dodgers starter Yu Darvish early in Game 3, knocking him out after only 1.2 innings pitched, thanks to a string of clutch hits. Houston eventually made an early four-run lead stand up, securing a 5-3 win to remain unbeaten at Minute Maid Park in the postseason.

The Astros took a 2-1 lead in the best-of-seven Fall Classic by becoming the eighth team in history to win at least seven home games in a postseason (7-0). The previous seven clubs won the World Series, and the Astros gave themselves the chance to become No. 8. Since the World Series moved permanently to the current 2-3-2 format in 1946, teams taking Game 3 at home for a 2-1 lead have won 11 of 16 times, and eight of the past nine.

"Four runs in any game is big. Four runs in the World Series is huge," Astros Manager A.J. Hinch said. "To get that kind of momentum started, get the crowd into it, and have a lead puts a ton of pressure on the other dugout. Obviously the quality of our at-bats tonight were incredible. That's more of our identity. That's what we're about. And to see it carry over from the last game to this game was welcome."

Darvish, who had allowed just two runs in 11.1 innings in two previous postseason starts and was 4-1 with a 2.16 ERA in six career starts at Minute Maid Park, gave up four runs and six hits.

"The fastball command wasn't there, and the slider was backing up," Dodgers Manager Dave Roberts said. "He really didn't have the feel and couldn't get any type of rhythm going. So right there you find yourself down, 4-0, after five outs — had to go to the 'pen to give us a chance to stay in that game."

Astros starter Lance McCullers Jr. held the Dodgers to three runs, four hits and four walks in 5.1 innings, pitching out of a bases-loaded jam in the third, allowing just one run.

Yuli Gurriel got the scoring started with a line-drive homer into the Crawford Boxes in the second, an inning in which the Astros batted around. Josh Reddick doubled and scored on a Marwin Gonzalez single, Evan Gattis walked and scored on a Brian McCann single, and Gonzalez scored on an Alex Bregman sacrifice fly to make it 4-0.

Leading 5-1 in the sixth, McCullers issued a leadoff walk to Corey Seager and a double to Justin Turner. The

right-hander was pulled after striking out Cody Bellinger and replaced by Brad Peacock. In only his second career save opportunity, Peacock allowed both Dodgers base runners to score on an RBI groundout by Yasiel Puig and a wild pitch — cutting the Astros' lead to 5-3 — but settled down and wound up throwing the final 3.2 innings to nail down his first career save.

"I thought they were going to go to [closer Ken] Giles or somebody," Peacock said after the game. "I'm glad they gave it to me. I was ready for the opportunity."

"The good part of our lineup is that we can score from anywhere. And we have [great] hitters up and down the lineup. The bottom of our order, especially [in] the big inning, put [together] good at-bat after good at-bat after good at-bat."

ASTROS MANAGER A.J. HINCH

GONZALEZ (TOP) DOUBLED IN A RUN IN THE SECOND INNING AND LATER SCORED TO STAKE THE ASTROS TO AN EARLY 4-0 LEAD. PEACOCK THEN TOSSED 3.2 HITLESS INNINGS OF RELIEF TO EARN THE SAVE AND NAIL DOWN THE VICTORY. REDDICK (FAR LEFT) SLID HOME AFTER A THROWING ERROR IN THE FIFTH INNING, GIVING HOUSTON ITS FIFTH RUN.

WORLD SERIES

GAME 4, OCTOBER 28
LOS ANGELES 6, HOUSTON 2

	1	2	3	4	5	6	7	8	9	R	H	E
LOS ANGELES	0	0	0	0	0	0	1	0	5	6	7	0
HOUSTON	0	0	0	0	0	1	0	0	1	2	2	0

WP: WATSON LP: GILES
HR: LAD: PEDERSON HOU: SPRINGER, BREGMAN

The Dodgers struck back in convincing fashion in Game 4, scoring five runs in the ninth inning, capped by a three-run homer by Joc Pederson, to beat the Astros and even the Series at two games apiece.

"They play extremely well [at Minute Maid Park], well, all the time, but we played them hard and things went well for us," Pederson said. "So it's encouraging that we have Kershaw [pitching for us] with the Series tied. We're in a good spot."

BREGMAN NOT ONLY PROVIDED THE ASTROS WITH A POWERFUL BAT THROUGH THE POSTSEASON, BUT HE ALSO MADE ONE DAZZLING PLAY AFTER ANOTHER AT THIRD BASE, INCLUDING NAILING AUSTIN BARNES AT HOME ON A GROUNDER IN THE SIXTH INNING. DODGERS ROOKIE BELLINGER (OPPOSITE) STARTED THE WORLD SERIES 0 FOR 13, BUT HE DOUBLED TO SPARK A RALLY TWICE LATE IN GAME 4 AND CAME AROUND TO SCORE BOTH TIMES.

Astros closer Ken Giles, who had allowed a run in five of six postseason outings this year entering Game 4, started the ninth inning of a tied game and allowed a single to Corey Seager and a walk to Justin Turner before Cody Bellinger put the Dodgers ahead with an RBI double. It marked the first time the Astros had trailed at home this postseason in 71 postseason innings.

Pederson's long homer to right off Joe Musgrove four batters later pushed the lead to 6-1. The only two hits the Astros managed were homers — by George Springer in the sixth and Alex Bregman in the ninth.

Teams that have won Game 4 to tie a Fall Classic have gone on to win the Series 24 of 44 times, including three of the past four in that scenario (2014 Giants, '13 Red Sox, '03 Marlins).

Dodgers starter Alex Wood, pitching for only the second time in 32 days, held the Astros without a hit through 5.2 innings before Springer blasted a solo homer to left to give the Astros a 1-0 lead and ignite the crowd. Springer became the first player to break up a World Series no-hit bid with a homer in the sixth inning or later.

"Wood is different in general — different arm angle, different mechanics, and we hadn't seen him before," Astros Manager A.J. Hinch said. "But it looked like he was teasing the strike zone a little bit. We were a little aggressive. He pitches very well down in the zone. He threw a well-pitched game."

Astros starter Charlie Morton gave up a leadoff single to Chris Taylor, who was thrown out trying to steal to end the first inning, and then retired the next 14 batters he faced, pumping the ball down in the zone consistently. He was pulled after giving up a one-out double in the seventh to Bellinger, who snapped an 0-for-13 skid in the World Series and came around to score the tying run on a Logan Forsythe single off Will Harris.

"Yeah, relief for sure," Bellinger said of getting two key doubles in the final three innings of the game. "I think everyone knows I was struggling. That's the beautiful thing about baseball — you can come out and help your team win the next day. And that's what I tried to do."

SPRINGER (OPPOSITE) BROKE UP WOOD'S NO-HIT BID WITH A HOME RUN IN THE SIXTH INNING. MORTON GAVE THE ASTROS A SOLID START, ALLOWING JUST ONE RUN THROUGH 6.1 INNINGS, BUT THE BULLPEN COULDN'T CLOSE OUT L.A.

"Facing those guys and really their whole lineup in general, you have to execute. If you don't execute, they're going to make you pay, as you've seen a little bit throughout the Series so far and watching them all year. They're a special lineup."

ALEX WOOD

WORLD SERIES

GAME 5, OCTOBER 29
HOUSTON 13, LOS ANGELES 12

	1	2	3	4	5	6	7	8	9	10	R	H	E
LOS ANGELES	3	0	0	1	3	0	1	1	3	0	12	14	1
HOUSTON	0	0	0	4	3	0	4	1	0	1	13	14	1

WP: MUSGROVE LP: JANSEN HR: LAD: BELLINGER, PUIG
HOU: GURRIEL, ALTUVE, SPRINGER, CORREA, McCANN

The never-say-die Astros pulled off the unthinkable in an epic Fall Classic matchup.

Alex Bregman hit a walk-off single to left field off Dodgers closer Kenley Jansen in the 10th inning to score pinch-runner Derek Fisher from second base, sending the Astros to a dramatic 13-12 victory.

"It's an unbelievable moment," Bregman said. "You dream about it as a little kid. To be living a dream, one win away from the World Series, is really special."

"It's hard to put into words all the twists and turns in that game, the emotion, doing it at home, in front of our home crowd," Astros Manager A.J. Hinch said.

Neither Dallas Keuchel nor Clayton Kershaw, a pair of Cy Young Award winners, made it through the fifth inning. Kershaw allowed six runs and four hits in 4.2 innings, and Keuchel allowed four runs (three earned) and five hits in 3.2 frames. Both bullpens got battered — Houston's gave up eight runs and nine hits in 6.1 innings, and Los Angeles' allowed seven runs and 10 hits in five innings.

After trading early blows, the Dodgers took an 8-7 lead in the seventh when Springer dove in center for a sinking line drive off the bat of Cody Bellinger and allowed it to go under his glove and roll to the wall for a triple that scored Enrique Hernandez. But Springer atoned for the misplay when he crushed the first pitch thrown by reliever Brandon Morrow in the bottom of the inning to tie the game.

After Springer's homer, Bregman singled and scored from first on a double by Jose Altuve to give the Astros their first lead, 9-8. Carlos Correa then hit a towering fly ball to left field that sneaked into the first rows of the Crawford Boxes for a two-run homer to put Houston ahead, 11-8. However, the scoring was not done yet.

The Dodgers cut the lead to 11-9 in the eighth on an RBI double by Corey Seager, but relievers Will Harris and Chris Devenski were able to end the threat.

Los Angeles turned the tables on Houston by coming back from a 12-9 deficit in the ninth inning. Yasiel Puig hit a two-run homer off Devenski, who was one strike away from ending the game when Chris Taylor shot an RBI single to center to tie it at 12.

"It was back and forth and you're trying to calm yourself down, calm your nerves," Devenski said. "All the excitement that was going on, all that stuff, just trying to go out there and slow the game down and do the best that you can."

Jansen, working his second inning, recorded two outs in the 10th before hitting Brian McCann with a pitch. When George Springer followed with a walk, Fisher replaced McCann at second as a pinch-runner and scored when Bregman hit a soft liner over Dodgers shortstop Corey Seager to win the game.

Fisher was appearing in just his fourth playoff game this year and didn't have an official at-bat in the postseason. Still, he was able to come off the bench and score the winning run.

"It was back and forth. Nonstop. It was unbelievable. The best game ever, for sure. Emotions are really high right now," Correa said.

"I'm sure everybody's pretty exhausted, emotionally and physically," Kershaw said. "It was a tough one. But you know what? We've still got a chance at this thing. I just lost my command a little bit and that's all it took."

ALL EYES WERE ON THE ASTROS AS THEY WERE DETERMINED TO PULL AWAY WITH A VICTORY IN THEIR FINAL HOME GAME OF THE SERIES. FORMER PRESIDENTS AND TEXAS NATIVES GEORGE H.W. BUSH AND HIS SON, GEORGE W. (LEFT), THREW THE FIRST PITCHES IN FRONT OF A CROWD OF 43,300 FANS. FISHER (ABOVE) DID NOT HAVE AN OFFICIAL POSTSEASON AT-BAT BUT STILL SCORED THE WINNING RUN FOR THE ASTROS.

SPRINGER'S SOLO SHOT (LEFT) TIED THE GAME IN THE SEVENTH AND ALTUVE (ABOVE) PUT THE ASTROS AHEAD SOON AFTER. CORREA'S HOME RUN (TOP LEFT) EXTENDED HOUSTON'S LEAD TO THREE RUNS BUT IT WASN'T OVER. TAYLOR (TOP RIGHT) TIED THE GAME IN THE NINTH WITH AN RBI SINGLE BUT BREGMAN'S WALK-OFF KNOCK FINALLY ENDED THE SEE-SAW MATCH.

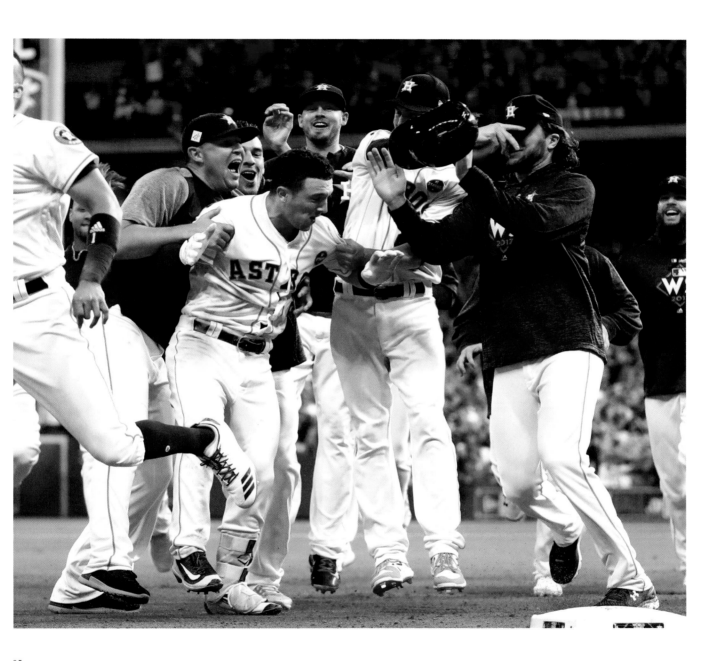

"It's an unbelievable moment. You dream about it as a little kid. To be living a dream, one win away from the World Series, is really special."

ALEX BREGMAN

WORLD SERIES

GAME 6, OCTOBER 31
LOS ANGELES 3, HOUSTON 1

	1	2	3	4	5	6	7	8	9	R	H	E
HOUSTON	0	0	1	0	0	0	0	0	0	1	6	0
LOS ANGELES	0	0	0	0	0	2	1	0	x	3	5	0

WP: WATSON LP: VERLANDER SV: JANSEN
HR: HOU: SPRINGER LAD: PEDERSON

SPRINGER (OPPOSITE) GOT THE OFFENSE STARTED WITH A SOLO SHOT IN THE THIRD INNING, BUT IT WAS THE ONLY RUN THAT THE ASTROS WOULD SCORE THAT NIGHT. PEDERSON'S HOMER IN THE SEVENTH GAVE THE DODGERS A 3-1 LEAD THAT THEY WOULDN'T RELINQUISH.

The Dodgers forced the first Fall Classic Game 7 in Dodger Stadium history by rallying to beat the Astros and Justin Verlander, 3-1, in front of an electrified sellout crowd at Chavez Ravine.

"It's how you play in the backyard of your house as a kid, imagine you're in Game 7 of the World Series," Houston shortstop Carlos Correa said.

"It's a dream come true to be part of it. We couldn't get the job done [in this game], so we're going to go out there and win the last. It's the last game of the season, so we want it to be the best."

Dodgers starting pitcher Rich Hill kept the game close, while the bullpen, freshened by a travel day, shut down the mighty Astros lineup. The L.A. offense did just enough, with Chris Taylor's RBI double keying a two-run sixth inning off Verlander and the rejuvenated Joc Pederson lofting his third homer of the Series, off reliever Joe Musgrove.

"We grinded the entire game," said Hill, removed after 4.2 innings when Manager Dave Roberts chose to go to his bullpen for the third time through the Houston lineup. "That's the makeup of this team the entire year."

Verlander, previously unbeaten in nine decisions since Houston acquired him, had allowed only one hit and was clinging to a slim lead provided by George Springer's homer in the third inning, his fourth of the Series and the 14th for the Astros, tying the 2002 Giants for the most in a Fall Classic.

"That's a good offensive team over there," Springer said. "One run is probably not going to hold up. It doesn't matter who's in the game. That's a good feeling right there to strike first, and we'll see what happens [next]."

Austin Barnes led off the sixth with a single. Verlander then hit Chase Utley with a pitch, Taylor doubled in one run and Corey Seager brought home another with a sacrifice fly.

Verlander struck out nine and allowed two runs on just three hits in six innings but suffered his first defeat with the Astros. At no point during the game did he allow himself the opportunity to think the Astros were going to finish it off.

"Absolutely not. No chance," Verlander said. "Not the way this Series has gone, not the way [the Dodgers'] lineup is. If we could have squeaked across one or two more, I might

have changed my mentality a little bit. I've played this game too long. What happened, that can happen to anyone. The best-hit ball that inning was a flyout to right field. That's why it's so hard to limit offense, especially in this Series."

Brandon Morrow took over for Hill and threw a scoreless inning. Kenta Maeda, who allowed a three-run homer to Jose Altuve in Game 5, pitched a scoreless frame as well.

And closer Kenley Jansen, who took the walk-off loss in Game 5 and had allowed two homers in the Series, retired all six batters he faced (three on strikeouts) for the biggest save of his career, using only 19 pitches. Tony Watson pitched one-third of an inning and was credited with the win.

"When you get hit in the mouth and you see the guy respond by wanting the baseball again and wanting another chance for redemption or whatever you want to term it, that's a good thing," said Roberts. "Our guys aren't afraid of the moment. And we've put a lot of time into this moment right here. So we're not done yet."

"I told the guys to be ready to play [tomorrow]. This is the biggest stage, the best stage, and the opportunity to win the World Series in Game 7. That was immediately my message when the last out was made."

ASTROS MANAGER A.J. HINCH

THE ASTROS RETURNED
TO DODGER STADIUM
WITH A 3-GAMES-TO-2
LEAD IN THE SERIES,
HOPING TO CLOSE IT
OUT. VERLANDER (LEFT)
STRUCK OUT NINE OVER
SIX INNINGS BUT WAS
HANDED HIS FIRST LOSS
OF THE POSTSEASON.

WORLD SERIES

GAME 7, NOVEMBER 1
HOUSTON 5, LOS ANGELES 1

	1	2	3	4	5	6	7	8	9	R	H	E
HOUSTON	2	3	0	0	0	0	0	0	0	5	5	0
LOS ANGELES	0	0	0	0	0	1	0	0	0	1	6	1

WP: MORTON LP: DARVISH HR: HOU: SPRINGER

The Astros, just four years removed from the low point of their bold rebuilding project, capped their remarkable turnaround and delivered a World Series championship to the city of Houston.

Houston, which pulled out heart-stopping wins in Games 2 and 5, took some drama out of Game 7 when it built an early 5-0 lead, capped by George Springer's two-run homer in the second off starter Yu Darvish, who recorded only five outs before being pulled from the game. The Astros kept the Dodgers at bay with a steady stream of relievers to finish piecing together the biggest 27 outs in franchise history.

Three pitches into the game, eventual Series MVP Springer doubled into the left-field corner. One pitch later, first baseman Cody Bellinger fielded Alex Bregman's bouncer in the hole and threw it into the Astros' dugout, putting Bregman at second and allowing Springer to score. He then stole third and scored on Jose Altuve's groundout.

Astros starting pitcher Lance McCullers Jr. helped himself with the bat in the second inning. Brian McCann worked a leadoff walk and was doubled to third by Marwin Gonzalez. With one out, McCullers drove McCann home on a groundout. Springer followed by crushing a 3-2 pitch into the seats in left-center, giving Houston a 5-0 advantage and becoming the first player to homer in four consecutive games of the same World Series.

From there, Astros Manager A.J. Hinch pieced together the outs. Brad Peacock threw two scoreless innings to hold the lead, and Charlie Morton fired four innings in relief to get the win, allowing one run and two hits.

When All-Star second baseman Altuve fielded a grounder off the bat of Corey Seager and threw to teammate Yuli Gurriel at first base in the ninth inning, the Astros had a franchise-defining 5-1 victory and their first-ever title.

"I got the last out for the Houston Astros becoming world champions," said Altuve. "It was a ground ball to me. I threw to first, and I [thought], 'this is the happiest moment in my life in baseball.'"

Los Angeles, appearing in the World Series for the first time since beating Oakland in 1988, used starters Clayton

Kershaw (four scoreless innings) and Alex Wood (two scoreless innings) in relief and closer Kenley Jansen in the seventh inning despite trailing by four runs.

"At the end of the day," said Kershaw, "we got beat by a team that probably deserved to win."

"It's hard to draw it up any better," Astros Manager A.J. Hinch said. "I don't care who we beat or where we beat them, I just want to be the last team standing, and we're taking this trophy, this championship vibe we've got, back to Houston. We'll forever be a championship city."

The franchise that began play in the National League in 1962 — and endured numerous postseason heartbreaks — won its first World Series just four years after losing a franchise-record 111 games during a rebuilding project that netted several contributors on this year's 101-win team.

"We had some rough years, but we stuck to our plan," said Astros General Manager Jeff Luhnow. "We did it. We knew we had a plan that could get us here, and we got it. [A] world championship."

Beating the Dodgers, who won an MLB-best 104 games, in a hard-fought Fall Classic brought the city of Houston its first major sports title in 22 years. L.A. finished the contest 1-for-13 with runners in scoring position

In the clubhouse after the game, Springer clutched the World Series trophy and said he couldn't wait to bring it back to Houston.

"It's a dream come true, and it's an honor [to win the World Series MVP Award]," Springer said. "But it's more about the people of Houston and our city. We're coming home champions!"

JUST FOUR YEARS AGO, THE HOUSTON ASTROS LOST 111 GAMES. BUT IN 2017, WITH A STABLE OF TALENTED INFIELDERS INCLUDING BREGMAN (OPPOSITE), THEY CLIMBED THE MOUNTAINTOP AND DELIVERED THE CITY ITS FIRST WORLD SERIES TITLE. MORTON CAME OUT OF THE BULLPEN TO EARN THE VICTORY IN THE DECISIVE GAME 7, NOTCHING HIS SECOND SERIES-CLINCHING WIN OF THE POSTSEASON.

"It's a dream come true, and it's an honor [to win the World Series MVP Award], but it's more about the people of Houston and our city. We're coming home champions!"

GEORGE SPRINGER

SPRINGER (OPPOSITE) WAS NAMED WORLD SERIES MVP AFTER HITTING FIVE FALL CLASSIC HOMERS, INCLUDING A KEY BLAST IN THE SECOND INNING OF GAME 7. ALTUVE LED THE CLUB WITH A .310 AVERAGE AND SEVEN HOME RUNS IN THE POSTSEASON.

SEASONED VETERANS SUCH AS JUSTIN VERLANDER, CARLOS BELTRÁN AND BRIAN McCANN EARNED THEIR FIRST WORLD SERIES CHAMPIONSHIP WITH HOUSTON'S VICTORY.

POSTSEASON STATS

NO.	PLAYER	W	L	ERA	WHIP	SO	SV
	PITCHERS						
47	CHRIS DEVENSKI	1	0	9.00	1.50	8	0
53	KEN GILES	0	2	11.74	2.22	10	2
44	LUKE GREGERSON	0	0	0.00	1.09	5	0
36	WILL HARRIS	0	0	2.25	1.75	3	0
60	DALLAS KEUCHEL	2	2	3.58	1.19	32	0
46	FRANCISCO LIRIANO	0	1	3.86	1.29	2	0
43	LANCE McCULLERS JR.	1	0	2.61	1.06	19	1
31	COLLIN McHUGH	0	0	4.50	0.83	7	0
50	CHARLIE MORTON	2	1	4.24	1.11	25	0
59	JOE MUSGROVE	1	0	8.10	1.05	3	0
41	BRAD PEACOCK	0	0	5.11	1.38	16	1
35	JUSTIN VERLANDER	4	1	2.21	0.82	38	0

NO.	PLAYER	AB	H	AVG	HR	RBI	OBP
	CATCHERS						
30	JUAN CENTENO	0	0	.000	0	0	.000
11	EVAN GATTIS	30	8	.267	1	3	.425
16	BRIAN McCANN	57	10	.175	1	7	.277
	INFIELDERS						
27	JOSE ALTUVE	71	22	.310	7	14	.388
2	ALEX BREGMAN	72	15	.208	4	10	.256
1	CARLOS CORREA	73	21	.288	5	14	.325
10	YULI GURRIEL	69	21	.304	2	8	.342
13	TYLER WHITE	0	0	.000	0	0	.000
	OUTFIELDERS						
15	CARLOS BELTRÁN	20	3	.150	0	1	.190
21	DEREK FISHER	0	0	.000	0	0	1.000
9	MARWIN GONZALEZ	61	11	.180	1	4	.275
3	CAMERON MAYBIN	7	2	.286	0	0	.375
22	JOSH REDDICK	65	11	.169	0	2	.229
4	GEORGE SPRINGER	72	21	.292	6	9	.386

MINUTE MAID PARK

Designed at the turn of the century, Minute Maid Park is Houston's first retractable-roof stadium, built as a replacement for the Astrodome in 2000. The stadium features natural grass and open-air baseball, something Houston had missed after playing in a dome since 1965. The 242-foot high retractable roof draws millions to the ballpark, as fans can experience the natural Texas atmosphere on crisp summer nights without having to worry about a rainout or the outdoor humidity.

A jewel in the crown of the downtown Houston skyline, Minute Maid Park ushered in a new era of Major League sports in the city, and the park itself has plenty of unique features. For years, the park featured Tal's Hill before its removal in 2016, a 90-foot incline in center field named after former Astros President Tal Smith. The grassy knoll often made catches in the outfield more difficult and acrobatic. And atop the left-field wall at Minute Maid Park stands a replica 19th century locomotive, which became a fast fan favorite in the inaugural season; the train provides a link to Houston's past at the Union Station site, and it whirrs around 800 feet of track each time an Astros player hits a home run. And with the young, powerful lineup now occupying the Houston dugout, fans can expect to see that train in action often, sending its celebratory toots into the Texas night.

WORLD SERIES CHAMPIONS 2017

2017 SEASON IN REVIEW

With another season in the books, baseball continues to be a steadying force for sports fans around the world. Milestones were achieved, both on the mound and at the plate, while fans experienced heartbreak and elation as their teams made the push toward the postseason. Rookies, in particular, took the baseball world by storm, breaking records left and right and proving that there's a plethora of talent to look forward to in the coming years. New traditions commenced while the game continued to make its global impact, and from April through October, the baseball world showed why the sport is one of a kind. The single-season record for total homers was set, and there were plenty of other great moments to remember.

APRIL

DALLAS DOMINATION

At the start of the 2017 season, the 2015 American League Cy Young Award winner showed that he could still shut down offenses two years later. Hurler **Dallas Keuchel** posted a 1.21 ERA and struck out 36 batters in April, good for Pitcher of the Month honors. The groundball specialist lasted at least seven innings in every start, never allowing more than two runs. In fact, Keuchel got off to a perfect 9–0 record to start the season, thanks in large part to his undefeated April in which the Astros won all but one of his first six starts.

BACK AND BREW

After a few seasons with the Blue Jays and Mariners, **Eric Thames** slipped into obscurity when he played in South Korea for three years. However, the Milwaukee Brewers signed him in the offseason and Thames responded by smashing 11 home runs for the month of April with a .345 batting average and 19 RBI.

STARTING WITH A BANG

Still just 24, **Bryce Harper** slugged his fifth straight Opening Day home run on April 3 for the Nationals.

MAY

MAYHEM

At age 23, shortstop **Carlos Correa** is younger than many rookies who made their Major League debuts this season. That didn't stop the 2015 AL Rookie of the Year from performing like a star in the early goings of the 2017 campaign. In May, Correa set career highs in numerous offensive categories for a single month, including home runs (seven), RBI (26) and total bases (68). He coupled this impressive power with a stellar .386/.457/.673 batting line, the best percentages in any such span since his debut. Correa was awarded AL Player of the Month honors for his efforts, and the Astros, consequently, began an 11-game winning streak in May, finishing with an outstanding 22-7 record.

HOUSTON HEAT

Right-hander **Lance McCullers Jr.** started six games for the red-hot Astros in May and got the win in four of them, posting a paltry 0.99 ERA and 0.85 WHIP, while averaging more than a strikeout per inning along the way, en route to garnering AL Pitcher of the Month honors. Meanwhile, his team finished the month with 22 wins as it maintained its spot in first place in the American League West.

CAN'T CATCH THIS

Reds speedster **Billy Hamilton** stole 18 bases for the month of May to register the third-best single-month stolen base total of his career.

SWEET STEPS

As the first professional baseball player ever to compete on Dancing with the Stars, two-time World Series champion **David Ross** garnered quite a bit of attention. Grandpa Rossy didn't disappoint, salsa dancing his way into second place.

JUNE

TOP OF THE TERROR

While the leadoff spot puts more emphasis on speed than power, outfielder **George Springer** breaks the mold. With his ability to get on base and smash extra base hits, the Astros center fielder is one of the most effective table setters in the game. On June 28, Springer showed baseball fans around the country just how impressive he can be, opening the game with a solo shot to become the fastest player to hit nine leadoff home runs to start a season. He blasted 11 home runs in June alone and scored 24 runs, bringing his totals through the first three months of the season to 24 homers and 63 runs scored.

ACES AT WORK

On June 2, former NL MVP and Cy Young Award winner **Clayton Kershaw** recorded the 2,000th strikeout of his career in just 277 games for the Dodgers, the second-fewest in MLB history behind Hall of Famer Randy Johnson. Nationals ace **Max Scherzer** accomplished the same K total on June 11, doing so in the third-fewest innings (1,784) in history, trailing Johnson and Pedro Martinez.

THE MAJOR LEAGUE MACHINE

Angels slugger **Albert Pujols** mashed the 600th home run of his career on June 3, becoming the ninth player ever to reach the mark and the fourth youngest overall. He is also the first to accomplish the feat with a grand slam, doing so off Twins ace Ervin Santana.

JULY

JUST ANOTHER JULY

While **Jose Altuve** might be diminutive in size, he's ferocious at the plate and on the basepaths, emerging yet again as an AL MVP candidate. Having led the Junior Circuit in batting average in two of the last three seasons, Altuve picked up right where he left off in 2017. In July, he took his hot hitting to new heights, registering a sizzling .485 batting average for the month, the highest mark for any player since Chipper Jones batted .500 in 2006. In the midst of the impressive stretch, he registered a career-long 19-game hitting streak and knocked 48 hits, one shy of the Astros' single-month record. Like Carlos Correa two months before him, Altuve took AL Player of the Month honors for his outstanding play.

THE VERDICT

Aaron Judge became the first rookie to win the Home Run Derby outright, slugging a total of 47 homers, good for second-most all time, in the July 10 competition in Miami. The Yankees phenom stunned fans and players alike when he hit both the centerfield glass and the roof at Marlins Park with his moonshots. He captured his title with 11 longballs in the finals to defeat Twins slugger Miguel Sano.

KILLER CONDOR

Chris Sale became the fastest pitcher in American League history to record 200 strikeouts in a season in his July 21 outing, doing it through only 141.1 innings and 20 starts. The Red Sox ace struck out Angels hitter Kole Calhoun and finished the day with nine K's.

AUGUST

QUICK STUDY

An integral part of the Astros' youth movement, third baseman **Alex Bregman** did his part to power the Astros' offense in August. The 23-year-old sophomore posted a .345 batting average and .395 OBP for the month, driving in 20 runners thanks to his ability to make hard contact. Showing off his speed, Bregman also swiped five bases and led the American League with three triples in the month. The passionate youngster showed clear growth throughout the season, plating nearly twice as many RBI after the All-Star break than before while raising his batting average by nearly 30 points. His hot bat helped the Astros stay atop the AL West during the dog days of summer.

SENIOR MOMENT

On August 4, 44-year-old **Bartolo Colon** became the oldest player to throw a complete game since Jamie Moyer did so with the Phillies in 2010. The veteran picked up his first win with the Minnesota Twins in the outing.

KLU-BOTIC

Indians ace **Corey Kluber** became the third pitcher in Major League history to log eight or more strikeouts in 13 consecutive starts on August 8 against the Rockies, joining the ranks of Hall of Famers Randy Johnson and Pedro Martinez. Kluber finished the complete-game effort with 11 K's.

ALL RHYS

On August 27, Phillies youngster **Rhys Hoskins** became the first player to hit his first 11 home runs in his first 18 games, and he started a 7-4-3 triple play for good measure.

SEPTEMBER

VETERAN COMPLEX

Sometimes, baseball fanatics say that one key addition can turn an above-average team into a World Series contender, and it's clear that **Justin Verlander** was the final piece to the puzzle that Houston needed. The second that he donned an Astros jersey, the veteran ace showed a renewed sense of fire and purpose. Verlander posted a 1.06 ERA in September to go along with a spotless 5-0 record, striking out 43 batters over 34 innings. The longtime Tigers stud was one of the best pitchers in baseball to close out the season, and the Astros rode his success to a 20-8 record in September to head into the playoffs on a hot streak. Their newfound ace continued to be a workhorse throughout the postseason, powering the Astros to a World Series title.

UNTOUCHABLE

The Cleveland Indians were practically unstoppable through September, winning 22 straight games, setting the American League record. During the club's incredible run, its hitters posted a .306/.385/.552 slash line and outscored opponents 142-37, while starting pitchers averaged a 1.77 ERA. It all came to an end on September 15 against the Royals, but the AL Central crown was sewn up by then.

MANNY MAGIC

Orioles slugger **Manny Machado** blasted a walk-off home run against the Yankees on September 5, which was his third game-winning shot in 19 days. He became the first player since Sammy Sosa in 1996 with that many walk-offs in as many days.

ROCKY MOUNTAIN HIGH

Rockies slugger **Charlie Blackmon** homered on September 29, driving in his 101st run of the season, which broke the record for most RBI from the leadoff spot in Major League history. Two days later, he finished the season with the NL batting title (.331).

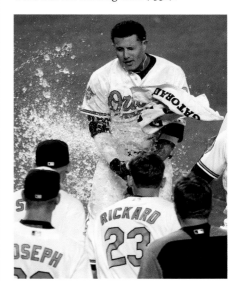

WHILE LONGORIA (LEFT) MAY HAVE HIT THE FIRST LONGBALL OF THE SEASON, THE HOUSTON ASTROS STILL RANKED SECOND IN THE BIG LEAGUES IN HOMERS.

HOME RUN RECORDS

Rays third baseman Evan Longoria was the first slugger to homer in the 2017 season, and his MLB counterparts followed suit from there. On September 19, Royals All-Star Alex Gordon broke MLB's single-season home run record. It was Gordon's eighth longball of the season, and the 5,694th in all of baseball in 2017. By the end of the season, sluggers blasted a total of 6,105 homers.

The New York Yankees led the Big Leagues in home runs (241), with the Houston Astros (238) and Texas Rangers (237)

rounding out the top three. Among the Bronx Bombers, rookie sensation Aaron Judge led with 52 dingers, the most by any rookie in history, passing the mark set by Mark McGwire in 1987.

Judge wasn't the only rookie blasting longballs, though. Cody Bellinger took the National League by storm and slugged 39 home runs for the Dodgers, while Hunter Renfroe, Josh Bell and Matt Davidson hit 26 apiece. The remaining top five combined for 117 homers.

FINAL 2017 STANDINGS

AMERICAN LEAGUE

EAST	W	L	GB
x Boston	93	69	–
w New York	91	71	2.0
Tampa Bay	80	82	13.0
Toronto	76	86	17.0
Baltimore	75	87	18.0

CENTRAL	W	L	GB
x Cleveland	102	60	–
w Minnesota	85	77	17.0
Kansas City	80	82	22.0
Chicago	67	95	35.0
Detroit	64	98	38.0

WEST	W	L	GB
x Houston	101	61	–
Los Angeles	80	82	21.0
Seattle	78	84	23.0
Texas	78	84	23.0
Oakland	75	87	26.0

NATIONAL LEAGUE

EAST	W	L	GB
x Washington	97	65	–
Miami	77	85	20.0
Atlanta	72	90	25.0
New York	70	92	27.0
Philadelphia	66	96	31.0

CENTRAL	W	L	GB
x Chicago	92	70	–
Milwaukee	86	76	6.0
St. Louis	83	79	9.0
Pittsburgh	75	87	17.0
Cincinnati	68	94	24.0

WEST	W	L	GB
x Los Angeles	104	58	–
w Arizona	93	69	11.0
w Colorado	87	75	17.0
San Diego	71	91	33.0
San Francisco	64	98	40.0

x Division winner; w Wild Card

CATEGORY LEADERS

AMERICAN LEAGUE

Batting Average	Jose Altuve, Houston	.346
Hits	Jose Altuve, Houston	204
Home Runs	Aaron Judge, New York	52
RBI	Nelson Cruz, Seattle	119
Stolen Bases	Whit Merrifield, Kansas City	34
Wins	Carlos Carrasco, Cleveland	18
	Corey Kluber, Cleveland	18
	Jason Vargas, Kansas City	18
ERA	Corey Kluber, Cleveland	2.25
Strikeouts	Chris Sale, Boston	308
Saves	Alex Colome, Tampa Bay	47

NATIONAL LEAGUE

Batting Average	Charlie Blackmon, Colorado	.331
Hits	Charlie Blackmon, Colorado	213
Home Runs	Giancarlo Stanton, Miami	59
RBI	Giancarlo Stanton, Miami	132
Stolen Bases	Dee Gordon, Miami	60
Wins	Clayton Kershaw, Los Angeles	18
ERA	Clayton Kershaw, Los Angeles	2.31
Strikeouts	Max Scherzer, Washington	268
Saves	Greg Holland, Colorado Kenley Jansen, Los Angeles	41

AMERICAN LEAGUE DIVISION SERIES

GAME 1, OCTOBER 5
HOUSTON 8, BOSTON 2

	1	2	3	4	5	6	7	8	9	R	H	E
BOSTON	0	1	0	1	0	0	0	0	0	2	8	0
HOUSTON	2	0	0	2	1	2	1	0	x	8	12	0

WP: VERLANDER LP: SALE HR: HOU: BREGMAN, ALTUVE (3)

The Astros opened their American League Division Series vs. the Red Sox with back-to-back homers in the first inning from Alex Bregman and Jose Altuve. After Boston tied it up, Marwin Gonzalez smacked a two-run double in the fourth off losing pitcher Chris Sale. Altuve hit two more solo shots to help put the game away and became the ninth player to tally three homers in a postseason game. Justin Verlander held the Red Sox to two runs in six innings for the victory, while Sale was charged with seven runs in five-plus frames.

GONZALEZ (LEFT) SMACKED AN RBI DOUBLE IN
THE FOURTH INNING THAT BROKE A 2-2 TIE. IN
VERLANDER'S (ABOVE) POSTSEASON DEBUT IN
AN ASTROS UNIFORM, THE RIGHTY TOSSED SIX
INNINGS OF TWO-RUN BALL.

ALTUVE (TOP) TIED A POSTSEASON RECORD BY HITTING THREE HOME RUNS IN A GAME. THE ASTROS OFFENSE DOMINATED SOX STARTER SALE (ABOVE), WHO SURRENDERED SEVEN RUNS ON NINE HITS THROUGH FIVE INNINGS. BREGMAN (FAR RIGHT) WAS THE FIRST TO GET TO HIM WITH A SOLO SHOT IN THE BOTTOM OF THE FIRST INNING.

GAME 2, OCTOBER 6
HOUSTON 8, BOSTON 2

	1	2	3	4	5	6	7	8	9	R	H	E
BOSTON	0	1	0	0	0	0	0	0	1	2	7	1
HOUSTON	2	0	2	0	0	4	0	0	x	8	12	0

WP: KEUCHEL LP: POMERANZ HR: HOU: CORREA, SPRINGER

Carlos Correa hit a two-run homer and a two-run double to lead the Astros as they defeated the Red Sox in Game 2 of the ALDS. With the win, Houston took a 2-games-to-none lead in the series. George Springer also homered, while Jose Altuve continued his postseason offensive tear with an RBI single and Evan Gattis contributed an RBI single. Houston's Dallas Keuchel yielded one run in 5.2 innings, striking out seven, and Boston's Drew Pomeranz was knocked out after giving up four runs in just two frames. David Price dealt 2.2 innings of scoreless relief for the Red Sox, whose only offense came on Jackie Bradley Jr.'s two RBI singles.

CORREA (RIGHT) PICKED UP TWO HITS ON THE DAY AND DROVE IN HALF OF THE ASTROS' RUNS, ALL OF THEM COMING ON TWO OUTS. KEUCHEL'S DOMINANCE IN THE REGULAR SEASON CARRIED INTO HIS ALDS START, AS HE STRUCK OUT SEVEN OVER 5.2 INNINGS, WHILE SURRENDERING ONLY ONE RUN.

"When you have two Cy Young winners in the front of your rotation, it gives you a lot of confidence, and we in the lineup know that a couple runs will be enough. So it's good to start with an early lead, and then Verlander and Keuchel are going to do the rest."

CARLOS CORREA

GAME 3, OCTOBER 8
BOSTON 10, HOUSTON 3

	1	2	3	4	5	6	7	8	9	R	H	E
HOUSTON	3	0	0	0	0	0	0	0	0	3	13	2
BOSTON	0	1	3	0	0	0	6	0	x	10	15	0

WP: KELLY LP: LIRIANO
HR: HOU: CORREA BOS: DEVERS, BRADLEY JR.

After being routed twice in Houston, the Red Sox went down early in a do-or-die Game 3 in Boston, with Carlos Correa homering in a three-run first. But Rafael Devers hit a go-ahead shot in the third, and starter-turned-reliever David Price turned in four key shutout innings. Hanley Ramirez went 4 for 4 with three RBI and Devers then added on, finishing with two hits and three RBI, and Jackie Bradley Jr.'s three-run homer put it away as part of a six-run seventh.

ALTUVE (ABOVE) PICKED UP THREE MORE HITS AT THE PLATE WHILE CORREA (RIGHT) SMASHED HIS SECOND LONGBALL OF THE SERIES. FOR THE RED SOX, BETTS SCORED A RUN WHILE MAKING SEVERAL STELLAR DEFENSIVE PLAYS IN THE OUTFIELD.

"We played with more of a sense of urgency. I know we understand it's kind of like a 'do or die or go home' situation. I think every game we should play with this sense of urgency."

MOOKIE BETTS

ALDS

GAME 4, OCTOBER 9
HOUSTON 5, BOSTON 4

	1	2	3	4	5	6	7	8	9	R	H	E
HOUSTON	1	1	0	0	0	0	0	2	1	5	12	0
BOSTON	1	0	0	0	2	0	0	0	1	4	9	1

WP: VERLANDER LP: SALE SV: GILES HR: HOU: BREGMAN
BOS: BOGAERTS, BENINTENDI, DEVERS

The Astros defeated the Red Sox in Game 4 of the ALDS, thanks to a go-ahead eighth-inning single from Josh Reddick, to move on to the ALCS for the first time in franchise history. Alex Bregman homered in the same frame to tie it up, and Justin Verlander delivered 2.2 innings of one-run ball in relief after starter Charlie Morton gave up two runs in 4.1 frames. Boston also called on its ace from the 'pen; Chris Sale gave up two runs in 4.2 innings after starter Rick Porcello yielded two runs in three frames. The Red Sox offense came on a Xander Bogaerts homer, which snapped an 0-for-14 skid, an Andrew Benintendi big fly and a Rafael Devers inside-the-parker. George Springer drove in an early run for Houston, and Carlos Beltran added insurance in the ninth.

ASTROS STARTER MORTON (LEFT) FANNED SIX OVER 4.1 INNINGS BEFORE HANDING THE BALL OVER TO VERLANDER, WHO PICKED UP HIS SECOND WIN OF THE SERIES IN 2.2 INNINGS OF ONE-HIT BALL. WITH THE VICTORY, THE ASTROS ADVANCED TO THE LEAGUE CHAMPIONSHIP SERIES FOR ONLY THE FIFTH TIME IN FRANCHISE HISTORY, AND FIRST TIME SINCE MOVING TO THE AMERICAN LEAGUE.

BOGAERTS (LEFT) TIED THE GAME WITH A SOLO SHOT, BUT REDDICK (OPPOSITE) PUT THE ASTROS UP WITH AN RBI SINGLE AND VERLANDER SETTLED DOWN AND HELD BOSTON TO ONLY ONE HIT.

WORLD SERIES CHAMPIONS
20 17

AMERICAN LEAGUE CHAMPIONSHIP SERIES

GAME 1, OCTOBER 13
HOUSTON 2, NEW YORK 1

	1	2	3	4	5	6	7	8	9	R	H	E
NEW YORK	0	0	0	0	0	0	0	0	1	1	5	0
HOUSTON	0	0	0	2	0	0	0	0	x	2	6	1

WP: KEUCHEL LP: TANAKA SV: GILES HR: NYY: BIRD

Dallas Keuchel struck out 10 and allowed just four hits and one walk over seven scoreless innings as the Astros topped the Yankees in Game 1 of the American League Championship Series. Yuli Gurriel and Carlos Correa each knocked in a run in the fourth inning, and Jose Altuve reached base on three hits and scored a run. Masahiro Tanaka allowed two runs on four hits and one walk in six innings for the Yanks, who got their lone run on a homer by Greg Bird with two outs in the ninth off Ken Giles.

DESPITE ALLOWING A SOLO SHOT FROM BIRD (LEFT) IN THE NINTH, GILES (OPPOSITE) STRUCK OUT FOUR TO NAIL DOWN THE SAVE FOR HOUSTON. TANAKA PITCHED SIX SOLID INNINGS, BUT IT WAS NOT ENOUGH AGAINST THE ASTROS OFFENSE.

"[Keuchel's] just special. He's special to watch. I love playing behind him. You've got to be ready for every single pitch knowing at some point you're going to get a ground ball. He's been consistent all year. That's what a Cy Young Award winner does."

CARLOS CORREA

KEUCHEL (OPPOSITE) AUTHORED ANOTHER DOMINANT START AGAINST THE YANKEES, STRIKING OUT 10 BATTERS OVER SEVEN SCORELESS INNINGS. CORREA AND GURRIEL PROVIDED RUN SUPPORT WHILE MARWIN GONZALEZ'S SHARP THROW FROM THE OUTFIELD PREVENTED NEW YORK FROM SCORING.

GAME 2, OCTOBER 14
HOUSTON 2, NEW YORK 1

	1	2	3	4	5	6	7	8	9	R	H	E
NEW YORK	0	0	0	0	1	0	0	0	0	1	5	0
HOUSTON	0	0	0	1	0	0	0	0	1	2	5	0

WP: VERLANDER LP: CHAPMAN HR: HOU: CORREA

Justin Verlander struck out 13 while earning his third win this postseason and Carlos Correa's double scored Jose Altuve for the game-winner of Game 2 of the ALCS. Correa, whose solo homer in the fourth was confirmed after a fan touched the ball, hit a liner to right-center against Yankees closer Aroldis Chapman in the ninth inning. Altuve appeared to be a sure out at the plate after rounding third, but catcher Gary Sanchez was unable to corral the throw. Verlander, who tossed a complete game, got some defensive help from Josh Reddick, who made a leaping catch at the fence in the third and then assisted as Brett Gardner was thrown out at third trying for a triple moments later.

STUCK IN A 1-1 DEADLOCK, ALTUVE (ABOVE) SCORED THE GAME-WINNING RUN ON A DOUBLE BY CORREA IN THE BOTTOM OF THE NINTH INNING. VERLANDER THREW A COMPLETE-GAME GEM, STRIKING OUT 13 WHILE ALLOWING ONLY ONE RUN.

"It's definitely up there, if not at the top ... It's definitely one of the most satisfying starts I've had in my career."

JUSTIN VERLANDER

GAME 3, OCTOBER 16
NEW YORK 8, HOUSTON 1

	1	2	3	4	5	6	7	8	9	R	H	E
HOUSTON	0	0	0	0	0	0	0	0	1	1	4	0
NEW YORK	0	3	0	5	0	0	0	0	x	8	7	1

WP: SABATHIA LP: MORTON HR: NYY: FRAZIER, JUDGE

The Yankees returned home and closed their deficit in the American League Championship Series to 2–1 thanks to a stellar game from Aaron Judge, who made a pair of spectacular catches and launched a three-run homer in the fourth to support six shutout innings from CC Sabathia. Todd Frazier got New York started with a three-run shot in the second off Astros starter Charlie Morton, who allowed seven runs in 3.2 innings.

THE YANKEES OFFENSE FINALLY CAME ALIVE, WITH FRAZIER (BOTTOM RIGHT) PUTTING NEW YORK ON THE BOARD WITH HIS FIRST CAREER POSTSEASON HOME RUN IN THE SECOND INNING. JUDGE (RIGHT) ADDED INSURANCE RUNS WITH HIS OWN THREE-RUN HOMER.

GAME 4, OCTOBER 17
NEW YORK 6, HOUSTON 4

	1	2	3	4	5	6	7	8	9	R	H	E
HOUSTON	0	0	0	0	0	3	1	0	0	4	3	0
NEW YORK	0	0	0	0	0	0	2	4	x	6	8	3

WP: GREEN LP: GILES SV: CHAPMAN HR: NYY: JUDGE

Runs were initially hard to come by in Game 4, with starters Lance McCullers Jr. and Sonny Gray dueling early, and Aaron Judge running New York out of a scoring opportunity with a blunder on the basepaths in the fourth. Houston finally broke through against Gray in the sixth, on Yuli Gurriel's bases-clearing double. But the Bombers had no intentions of going quietly. Judge atoned for his error with a homer, and the Yankees piled on from there, batting around in the eighth to tie the score and take the lead, ensuring that the ALCS would head back to Houston.

McCULLERS JR. (ABOVE) PITCHED SIX SOLID INNINGS BEFORE TURNING IT OVER TO THE HOUSTON BULLPEN, WHICH WAS UNABLE TO HOLD OFF THE YANKEES OFFENSE. JUDGE (TOP RIGHT) AND SANCHEZ COMBINED FOR FIVE RBI.

"That ballpark is alive. It was unbelievable.
That stadium was rocking, the fans were going crazy.
I didn't know what to do after I touched home plate.
That's why we play this game, for a moment like that."

AARON JUDGE

GAME 5, OCTOBER 18
NEW YORK 5, HOUSTON 0

	1	2	3	4	5	6	7	8	9	R	H	E
HOUSTON	0	0	0	0	0	0	0	0	0	0	4	1
NEW YORK	0	1	1	0	2	0	1	0	x	5	10	1

WP: TANAKA LP: KEUCHEL HR: NYY: SANCHEZ

Aaron Judge delivered an RBI double and scored on Didi Gregorius' RBI single that chased Astros ace Dallas Keuchel in the fifth inning, while Masahiro Tanaka fired seven shutout frames to help the Yankees take a 3-2 lead in the ALCS. The Yanks, who won their third straight in the series to go 6-0 at home this postseason, moved just one win away from their first World Series appearance since 2009. Tanaka's two starts of seven shutout innings tie Roger Clemens and Whitey Ford for the most in a single postseason by a Yankees pitcher. Keuchel, who is the first pitcher to record seven-plus strikeouts in each of his first five career postseason starts, was charged with four runs over 4.2 innings to go with his eight K's.

CORREA (OPPOSITE) AND GEORGE SPRINGER (DIRECTLY ABOVE) PICKED UP TWO OF THE FOUR ASTROS HITS OF THE NIGHT. TANAKA (TOP RIGHT) THREW A SCORELESS GEM, STRIKING OUT EIGHT IN SEVEN INNINGS. JUDGE CONTINUED HIS HOT HITTING AT HOME WITH AN RBI DOUBLE IN THE THIRD.

GAME 6, OCTOBER 20
HOUSTON 7, NEW YORK 1

	1	2	3	4	5	6	7	8	9	R	H	E
NEW YORK	0	0	0	0	0	0	0	1	0	1	7	1
HOUSTON	0	0	0	0	3	0	0	4	x	7	8	0

WP: VERLANDER LP: SEVERINO
HR: NYY: JUDGE HOU: ALTUVE

Justin Verlander delivered seven scoreless innings — helped by a spectacular run-saving catch from George Springer — and the Astros broke out of an offensive funk to force a Game 7. Luis Severino carried a no-hitter into the fourth inning, but Houston ended the pitchers' duel in the fifth on Brian McCann's RBI double and Jose Altuve's two-run single. Altuve, the MLB batting champ, also homered as the Astros broke it open with a four-run eighth. Aaron Judge put the Yankees on the board with a 425-foot blast in the eighth, becoming the fourth rookie to hit four home runs in a postseason.

YULI GURRIEL (ABOVE) SCORED AN INSURANCE RUN FOR THE ASTROS, WHO FED OFF THE HOME CROWD ENERGY TO SCORE MORE RUNS THAN IN THE PREVIOUS THREE GAMES COMBINED.

ALTUVE (RIGHT) HIT HIS
FIRST HOME RUN OF THE
SERIES OFF DAVID
ROBERTSON IN THE
EIGHTH, WHILE DRIVING
IN THREE RUNS.
VERLANDER WAS
MASTERFUL YET AGAIN,
SHUTTING OUT THE
YANKEES IN SEVEN
INNINGS OF WORK.

"He's been everything that we could have hoped for and more. This guy prepares. He rises to the moment. He's incredibly focused, locked in during games and emptied his tank tonight. I'm so proud of him, because I know how much it means to him … I hope we get to see him pitch again."

ASTROS MANAGER A.J. HINCH ON JUSTIN VERLANDER

GAME 7, OCTOBER 21
HOUSTON 4, NEW YORK 0

	1	2	3	4	5	6	7	8	9	R	H	E
NEW YORK	0	0	0	0	0	0	0	0	0	0	3	0
HOUSTON	0	0	0	1	3	0	0	0	x	4	10	0

WP: MORTON LP: SABATHIA SV: McCULLERS JR.
HR: HOU: GATTIS, ALTUVE

Houston earned a trip to the World Series for the second time in franchise history, and for the first time as an American League team. The Astros again stifled the Yanks at home, where they stayed unbeaten this postseason. Charlie Morton threw five innings of two-hit ball, and Lance McCullers Jr. gave up just one hit in four frames. Evan Gattis and Jose Altuve went deep, while Brian McCann plated a pair. Justin Verlander took home ALCS MVP honors.

SABATHIA (LEFT) ALLOWED ONLY ONE RUN, BUT THAT'S ALL HOUSTON NEEDED IN GAME 7. THE ASTROS OFFENSE BROKE OUT IN THE FIFTH INNING AND SCORED THREE RUNS OFF TOMMY KAHNLE, INCLUDING AN RBI DOUBLE BY BRIAN McCANN (OPPOSITE).

"As a team, we set the tone on doing things right. We got together and we created an environment in the clubhouse, a fun environment, and I'm proud. I'm proud of the whole team. Everybody went out there and did their job. We have gone through ups and downs, but we have been able to overcome the tough situations."

CARLOS BELTRÁN

MORTON (LEFT) HELD THE
YANKEES TO ONLY TWO
HITS IN FIVE SCORELESS
INNINGS, BEFORE
McCULLERS JR. PITCHED
FOUR INNINGS OF RELIEF.

BIRTH OF THE ASTROS

Up until 1961, Texas was without a Major League baseball franchise, and Houston's only professional ball club was the Buffaloes, a Minor League team. But on October 17, 1960, the National League granted an expansion franchise to the Houston Sports Association, and with the expansion draft in 1961, the Colt .45s were born. They played their first Major League game on April 10, 1962, and defeated the Chicago Cubs, 11-2. Three seasons later, ownership renamed the club "The Astros," a nod to Houston's role as the headquarters for the U.S. space program, and they moved into the Astrodome, the nation's first domed sports stadium.

Before divisions were established in baseball's two leagues, the Astros never finished better than eighth in the National League, and after the formation of the NL West in 1969, they didn't finish higher than third place until '79. The club had its first true infusion of talent that season, finishing just a game-and-a-half behind the first-place Reds, with players like J.R. Richard and Joe Niekro setting franchise records on the mound. A year later, they claimed their first NL West title after winning 93 games behind the dynamic arm of Nolan Ryan, but they ultimately lost in the NLCS. Ryan posted a 1.69 ERA in the 1981 campaign, but the Astros would lose in the NLDS, and would fall to the Mets in the '86 NLCS a few years later before Ryan departed for the Texas Rangers in '89.

With the arrival of sluggers Jeff Bagwell, Craig Biggio and Lance Berkman, the Astros saw a resurgence in the late 1990s. Aces Roy Oswalt and Roger Clemens joined the fray in the early 2000s, and the Astros would make their first and only World Series appearance in '05, where they were swept by an upstart Chicago White Sox team. It took until this latest round of young talent, ushered in by General Manager Jeff Luhnow, for the Astros to fully realize their potential and secure that elusive World Series title, the first in franchise history.

ASTROS POSTSEASON HISTORY

ASTROS CLOSER BILLY WAGNER FINISHED THE 1999 REGULAR SEASON WITH 39 SAVES AND PICKED UP HIS FIRST ALL-STAR NOD AS HOUSTON WON 97 GAMES AND PLAYED IN THE NLDS AGAINST THE ATLANTA BRAVES.

1980

NLCS

PHILADELPHIA PHILLIES 3
HOUSTON ASTROS 2

Oct. 7 Astros 1 at Phillies 3
Oct. 8 Astros 7 at Phillies 4
Oct. 10 Phillies 0 at Astros 1
Oct. 11 Phillies 5 at Astros 3
Oct. 12 Phillies 8 at Astros 7

1981

NLDS

LOS ANGELES DODGERS 3
HOUSTON ASTROS 2

Oct. 6 Dodgers 1 at Astros 3
Oct. 7 Dodgers 0 at Astros 1
Oct. 9 Astros 1 at Dodgers 6
Oct. 10 Astros 1 at Dodgers 2
Oct. 11 Astros 0 at Dodgers 4

1986

NLCS

NEW YORK METS 4
HOUSTON ASTROS 2

Oct. 8 Mets 0 at Astros 1
Oct. 9 Mets 5 at Astros 1
Oct. 11 Astros 5 at Mets 6
Oct. 12 Astros 3 at Mets 1
Oct. 14 Astros 1 at Mets 2
Oct. 15 Mets 7 at Astros 6

1997

NLDS
ATLANTA BRAVES 3
HOUSTON ASTROS 0

    Sept. 30 Astros 1 at Braves 2
    Oct. 1 Astros 3 at Braves 13
    Oct. 3 Braves 4 at Astros 1

1998

NLDS
SAN DIEGO PADRES 3
HOUSTON ASTROS 1

    Sept. 29 Padres 2 at Astros 1
    Oct. 1 Padres 4 at Astros 5
    Oct. 3 Astros 1 at Padres 2
    Oct. 4 Astros 1 at Padres 6

1999

NLDS
ATLANTA BRAVES 3
HOUSTON ASTROS 1

    Oct. 5 Astros 6 at Braves 1
    Oct. 6 Astros 1 at Braves 5
    Oct. 8 Braves 5 at Astros 3
    Oct. 9 Braves 7 at Astros 5

2001

NLDS
ATLANTA BRAVES 3
HOUSTON ASTROS 0

    Oct. 9 Braves 7 at Astros 4
    Oct. 10 Braves 1 at Astros 0
    Oct. 12 Astros 2 at Braves 6

RANDY JOHNSON WAS ONLY IN HOUSTON FOR THE SECOND HALF OF THE 1998 SEASON, BUT HE MADE HIS MARK, GOING 10-1 WITH A 1.28 ERA IN 11 REGULAR-SEASON STARTS. HE AUTHORED A 1.93 ERA OVER A PAIR OF NLDS STARTS AGAINST THE PADRES THAT YEAR.

2004

NLDS

HOUSTON ASTROS 3
ATLANTA BRAVES 2

Oct. 6 Astros 9 at Braves 3
Oct. 7 Astros 2 at Braves 4
Oct. 9 Braves 5 at Astros 8
Oct. 10 Braves 6 at Astros 5
Oct. 11 Astros 12 at Braves 3

NLCS

ST. LOUIS CARDINALS 4
HOUSTON ASTROS 3

Oct. 13 Astros 7 at Cardinals 10
Oct. 14 Astros 4 at Cardinals 6
Oct. 16 Cardinals 2 at Astros 5
Oct. 17 Cardinals 5 at Astros 6
Oct. 18 Cardinals 0 at Astros 3
Oct. 20 Astros 4 at Cardinals 6
Oct. 21 Astros 2 at Cardinals 5

2005

NLDS

HOUSTON ASTROS 3
ATLANTA BRAVES 1

Oct. 5 Astros 10 at Braves 5
Oct. 6 Astros 1 at Braves 7
Oct. 8 Braves 3 at Astros 7
Oct. 9 Braves 6 at Astros 7

NLCS

HOUSTON ASTROS 4
ST. LOUIS CARDINALS 2

Oct. 12 Astros 3 at Cardinals 5
Oct. 13 Astros 4 at Cardinals 1
Oct. 15 Cardinals 3 at Astros 4
Oct. 16 Cardinals 1 at Astros 2
Oct. 17 Cardinals 5 at Astros 4
Oct. 19 Astros 5 at Cardinals 1

AFTER STARTING THE 2005 SEASON 15-30, THE ASTROS
STORMED TO A WILD CARD BERTH AND REACHED THE
WORLD SERIES FOR THE FIRST TIME IN FRANCHISE
HISTORY BY DEFEATING THE CARDINALS IN THE NLCS.
THE CLUB BECAME THE FIRST TEAM IN OVER 90 YEARS
TO MAKE THE POSTSEASON AFTER FALLING 15 GAMES
BELOW .500 AT ANY POINT IN THE SEASON.

WORLD SERIES

CHICAGO WHITE SOX 4

HOUSTON ASTROS 0

    Oct. 22 Astros 3 at White Sox 5

    Oct. 23 Astros 6 at White Sox 7

    Oct. 25 White Sox 7 at Astros 5

    Oct. 26 White Sox 1 at Astros 0

The Astros began 2005 with a list of problems that suggested this was going to be a long, and likely unsuccessful, season. Lance Berkman was out for a month following offseason knee surgery. Jeff Bagwell struggled through a painful first month before deciding it was time to go on the disabled list.

However, Houston advanced to the World Series for the first time in franchise history after defeating the Cardinals in a rematch of the 2004 NLCS. The White Sox swept the Astros in four games to claim their first World Series since 1917. The Astros won the Wild Card for the second season in a row, finishing in second place in the NL Central division. The club started the season with a 2-21 record on the road, and overcame a 15-30 start on May 24 to become the first team since the 1914 Boston Braves to make the postseason after falling to 15 games below .500.

2015

WILD CARD GAME

HOUSTON ASTROS 1

NEW YORK YANKEES 0

    Oct. 6 Astros 3 at Yankees 0

ALDS

KANSAS CITY ROYALS 3

HOUSTON ASTROS 2

    Oct. 8 Astros 5 at Royals 2

    Oct. 9 Astros 4 at Royals 5

    Oct. 11 Royals 2 at Astros 4

    Oct. 12 Royals 9 at Astros 6

    Oct. 14 Astros 2 at Royals 7

THE ASTROS WATCHED FROM THE DUGOUT DURING GAME 1 OF THE 2005 WORLD SERIES AGAINST THE WHITE SOX IN WHAT WAS HOUSTON'S FIRST AND ONLY FALL CLASSIC APPEARANCE UNTIL THIS YEAR'S SQUAD WON IT ALL.

LED BY EVENTUAL AL CY YOUNG WINNER DALLAS KEUCHEL (RIGHT), THE 2015 ASTROS DEFEATED THE YANKEES 3-0 IN THE AMERICAN LEAGUE WILD CARD GAME. THEY WOULD BEAT THOSE SAME BRONX BOMBERS IN A HARD-FOUGHT ALCS TO REACH THE WORLD SERIES TWO YEARS LATER.

WORLD SERIES CHAMPIONS 2017

HOW THE ASTROS WERE BUILT

The Houston Astros built this championship team over the last decade through high draft picks, smart free agent signings and key trades, eventually turning into the recipe for 2017 success.

Houston would not have made the World Series without two homegrown stars on the mound — 2015 American League Cy Young Award winner Dallas Keuchel and 2012 first-round pick Lance McCullers Jr. In the bullpen, relievers like Chris Devenski, Will Harris, Brad Peacock and Ken Giles came into their own after spending multiple seasons excelling with the club. To top it off, in a blockbuster move, the club added former Tigers ace Justin Verlander at the waiver trade deadline, giving them a veteran pitcher who dominated down the stretch.

The best lineup in the Majors was built on a bedrock of impressive scouting: First baseman Yuli Gurriel and second baseman Jose Altuve were signed as international free agents out of Cuba and Venezuela, respectively, while shortstop Carlos Correa and third baseman Alex Bregman were both first round picks in the 2012 and '15 Drafts. In the outfield, George Springer and Marwin Gonzalez have been on the Astros for their entire careers, while Josh Reddick arrived through free agency. Finally, behind the plate (and often at DH), the duo of Evan Gattis and Brian McCann guided Houston's pitching staff to success. This group may have come from far and wide, but it came together in stellar fashion to bring Houston its first ever World Series title this season.

DRAFT

ALEX BREGMAN	1st round, 2015
CARLOS CORREA	1st round, 2012
J.D. DAVIS	3rd round, 2014
DEREK FISHER	1st round, 2014
TONY KEMP	5th round, 2013
DALLAS KEUCHEL	7th round, 2009
LANCE McCULLERS JR.	1st round, 2012
A.J. REED	2nd round, 2014
GEORGE SPRINGER	1st round, 2011
TYLER WHITE	33rd round, 2013

FREE AGENCY

JOSE ALTUVE	International signing (2007)
CARLOS BELTRÁN	1 year (2017)
JUAN CENTENO	Minor League contract (2016)
MICHAEL FELIZ	International signing (2010)
LUKE GREGERSON	3 years (2014)
REYMIN GUDUAN	International signing (2010)
YULI GURRIEL	International signing (2016)
CHARLIE MORTON	2 years (2017)
JOSH REDDICK	4 years (2017)
TONY SIPP	3 years (2016)

TRADES

TYLER CLIPPARD	From CWS for cash (2017)
CHRIS DEVENSKI	From CWS with Matt Heidenreich and Blair Walters for Brett Myers (2012)
MIKE FIERS	From MIL with Carlos Gomez for Josh Hader, Adrian Houser, Brett Phillips and Domingo Santana (2015)
EVAN GATTIS	From ATL with James Hoyt for Mike Foltynewicz, Rio Ruiz and Andrew Thurman (2015)
KEN GILES	From PHI with Jonathan Arauz for Mark Appel, Harold Arauz, Thomas Eshelman, Brett Oberholtzer and Vince Velasquez (2015)
MARWIN GONZALEZ	From BOS for Marco Duarte (2011)
WILL HARRIS	Off waivers from ARI (2014)
JAMES HOYT	From ATL with Evan Gattis for Mike Foltynewicz, Rio Ruiz and Andrew Thurman (2015)
FRANCISCO LIRIANO	From TOR for Norichika Aoki and Teoscar Hernandez (2017)
JAKE MARISNICK	From MIA with Francis Martes and Colin Moran for Austin Wates, Jarred Cosart and Enrique Hernandez (2014)
FRANCIS MARTES	From MIA with Jake Marisnick and Colin Moran for Austin Wates, Jarred Cosart and Enrique Hernandez (2014)
CAMERON MAYBIN	Off waivers from LAA (2017)
BRIAN McCANN	From NYY for Albert Abreu and Jorge Guzman (2016)
COLLIN McHUGH	Off waivers from COL (2013)
COLIN MORAN	From MIA with Jake Marisnick and Francis Martes for Austin Wates, Jarred Cosart and Enrique Hernandez (2014)
JOE MUSGROVE	From TOR with Francisco Cordero, Ben Francisco, Carlos Perez, David Rollins, Asher Wojciechowski and Kevin Comer for David Carpenter, J.A. Happ and Brandon Lyon (2012)
BRAD PEACOCK	From OAK with Chris Carter and Max Stassi for Jed Lowrie and Fernando Rodriguez (2013)
MAX STASSI	From OAK with Chris Carter and Brad Peacock for Jed Lowrie and Fernando Rodriguez (2013)
JUSTIN VERLANDER	From DET with Juan Ramirez for Daz Cameron, Franklin Perez and Jake Rogers (2017)

A.J. HINCH
MANAGER

In his third year managing the club, Hinch has guided the Astros to their third winning season in a row, en route to the AL West division title and their second postseason appearance in three years.

14

JOSE ALTUVE
SECOND BASE

A five-time All-Star and three-time American League batting champion, Altuve, an MVP candidate, tied a postseason record when he smashed three home runs during Game 1 of the Division Series.

27

CARLOS BELTRÁN
DESIGNATED HITTER

In his 20th season, the stalwart veteran and nine-time All-Star enjoyed a solid season in the DH role. His RBI double in Game 4 of the ALDS was the decisive factor in the Astros' series clinch.

15

ALEX BREGMAN
THIRD BASE

In only his second year in the Big Leagues, Bregman enjoyed a power surge at the plate and tied the Astros' extra-base hit streak record. He ranked first in the AL in fielding percentage at third base.

2

JUAN
CENTENO
CATCHER

Signed as a free agent during the offseason, Centeno earned a spot on the Astros postseason roster as a backup catcher, largely due to his strong arm and stellar defense behind the plate.

30

TYLER
CLIPPARD
PITCHER

Originally drafted by the Yankees in 2003, Clippard was traded to the Astros in the middle of the 2017 season. A two-time All-Star, Clippard held batters to a .120 average when pitching at Minute Maid Park.

19

CARLOS CORREA
SHORTSTOP

The 2015 American League Rookie of the Year enjoyed an All-Star campaign in 2017. Despite missing part of the season due to injury, he still ranked 10th in the Junior Circuit in OPS and ninth in WAR.

1

J.D.
DAVIS
THIRD BASE

A third-round selection in the 2014 Draft, Davis slugged four home runs in his first season in Houston.

28

CHRIS
DEVENSKI
PITCHER

After being chosen for his first AL All-Star team back in July, Devenski reached triple-digit strikeout numbers as a reliever for the second season in a row, and ranked sixth in the American League in holds in 2017.

47

MICHAEL FELIZ
PITCHER

In his third season pitching for the Astros, Feliz tallied 70 strikeouts over 48 innings and logged a pair of holds.

45

MIKE FIERS
PITCHER

Fiers posted a 2.59 ERA through 10 starts in June and July, and finished the season with the second-highest strikeout total of his career.

54

DEREK FISHER
OUTFIELD

In Fisher's Major League debut back in June, he homered and laced an RBI single in the same inning. He ended the season with five longballs and was named one of two Astros' Prospects of the Year.

21

EVAN GATTIS
CATCHER

Despite missing parts of the season due to injuries, Gattis tied a career high in batting average in his 2017 campaign, hitting .263 with 12 home runs in his role as a backup catcher for Brian McCann.

11

KEN GILES
PITCHER

In Giles' second season in Houston, his career-high 34 saves ranked fourth in the American League. He held batters to a mere .198 average out of the bullpen while pitching to a 0.84 ERA at home.

53

MARWIN
GONZALEZ
UTILITY

Gonzalez reached career highs
in various offensive categories
in 2017, including average, OPS,
home runs, RBI and runs scored.
The utilityman has played every
position in his career, aside from
pitcher and catcher.

9

LUKE GREGERSON
PITCHER

In his ninth season pitching in the Big Leagues, Gregerson averaged more than a strikeout per inning in 65 relief appearances for the Astros, tallying 10 K's through the final month of the regular season.

44

REYMIN GUDUAN
PITCHER

In his first year in the Big Leagues, Guduan averaged a strikeout per inning through 22 games in the regular season.

64

YULI GURRIEL
FIRST BASE

Gurriel picked up AL Rookie of the Month honors in July, and finished the season ranked 12th in batting average, leading all AL rookies. He was tied for the lead in doubles among all first basemen.

10

WILL HARRIS
PITCHER

Harris followed up his All-Star 2016 season with another strong campaign from the bullpen, ranking 11th in the American League in holds and averaging more than a strikeout per inning.

36

JAMES HOYT
PITCHER

After debuting in 2016, Hoyt doubled his number of innings pitched and strikeout totals. He posted a 1.50 ERA in August and did not allow a run in five appearances in the final month of the season.

51

TONY KEMP
OUTFIELD

A fifth-round selection in the 2013 Draft, Kemp provided depth in the outfield while playing solid defense for Houston.

18

DALLAS KEUCHEL
PITCHER

A former AL Cy Young Award winner and three-time Gold Glover, Keuchel was named to his second All-Star team in 2017 and ranked ninth in the AL in wins. He opened the ALCS with a dominant win over New York.

60

FRANCISCO LIRIANO
PITCHER

A starter-turned-reliever, Liriano joined the Astros at the trade deadline and made 20 relief appearances. The 12-year veteran limited lefties to a miniscule .655 OPS in 2017.

46

JAKE MARISNICK
OUTFIELD

Marisnick smashed a career-high 16 home runs, with 12 of them off righties, and posted a career-best .496 slugging percentage in 2017.

6

FRANCIS MARTES
PITCHER

In his first season in the Big Leagues, Martes struck out 69 batters over 54.1 innings and held right-handed batters to a .239 average.

58

CAMERON MAYBIN
OUTFIELD

Maybin joined the Astros in September and finished the season ranked second in the AL in stolen bases. He also tied a career high in home runs and racked up the most walks of his career in 2017.

3

BRIAN McCANN
CATCHER

A six-time Silver Slugger, McCann recorded his 12th consecutive season in which he smashed at least 15 home runs. He also posted an OPS over .750 for the third year in a row.

16

LANCE McCULLERS JR.

PITCHER

McCullers Jr. made his first All-Star appearance after an impressive May showing, in which he posted a 0.99 ERA. The youngster notched 132 K's in 2017.

43

COLLIN McHUGH
PITCHER

Although he missed part of the season due to injury, McHugh averaged nearly a strikeout per inning and held righties to a .218 batting average.

31

COLIN MORAN
INFIELD

A first-round draft pick in 2013, Moran, who missed much of the season due to injury, was still able to slug a pair of extra-base hits and drive in three runs over seven games.

38

CHARLIE MORTON
PITCHER

Signed as a free agent in the offseason, Morton struck out a career-high 163 batters and ranked ninth in the AL in wins with 14. His win total was tied for the most among the Astros starting rotation.

50

JOE MUSGROVE
PITCHER

Musgrove shifted from a starter to the bullpen midway through the season and excelled in the role, posting a measly 1.44 ERA as a reliever, while allowing only five walks in 23 relief appearances.

59

BRAD PEACOCK

PITCHER

Peacock earned a spot in the rotation at the end of May after allowing only four runs in 13 relief appearances. He finished the season with 161 strikeouts and held righties to a mere .173 average.

41

JOSH
REDDICK
OUTFIELD

Reddick joined the Astros prior to the start of the season and reached career highs in slugging percentage and batting average in 2017, ranking third among all outfielders in the latter category.

22

A.J. REED
FIRST BASE

Drafted by the Astros in the second round in 2014, Reed, a Minor League All-Star, filled in at first base during the summer.

23

TONY SIPP
PITCHER

Sipp posted the second-lowest walk total of his career in 2017, and recorded a 1.69 ERA in the final month of the season.

29

GEORGE SPRINGER
OUTFIELD

Springer experienced a breakout season in his fourth year with the team, garnering his first All-Star nod. He was second among Big Leaguers in runs scored from the leadoff position and third in homers.

4

MAX STASSI
CATCHER

As a backup catcher, Stassi hit two home runs and scored five times in 2017. Behind the plate, the backstop did not allow a passed ball in more than 64 innings.

12

JUSTIN VERLANDER
PITCHER

Traded from the Tigers at the end of August, Verlander posted a 1.06 ERA in five starts for the Astros. The former pitching Triple Crown winner ranked in the top 10 in the AL in wins, WHIP, strikeouts and ERA.

35

TYLER WHITE
FIRST BASE

White slugged .525 in the 2017 regular season. He had the second multi-homer game of his career on Aug. 4, during which he drove in five runs, scored three times and picked up four hits.

13

REGULAR-SEASON STATS

NO.	PLAYER	B/T	W	L	ERA	SO	BB	SV	BIRTHDATE	BIRTHPLACE
PITCHERS										
19	TYLER CLIPPARD	R/R	2	8	4.77	72	31	5	2/14/85	Lexington, KY
47	CHRIS DEVENSKI	R/R	8	5	2.68	100	26	4	11/13/90	Cerritos, CA
45	MICHAEL FELIZ	R/R	4	2	5.63	70	22	0	6/28/93	Azua, D.R.
54	MIKE FIERS	R/R	8	10	5.22	146	62	0	6/15/85	Hollywood, FL
53	KEN GILES	R/R	1	3	2.30	83	21	34	9/20/90	Albuquerque, NM
44	LUKE GREGERSON	L/R	2	3	4.57	70	20	1	5/14/84	Park Ridge, IL
64	REYMIN GUDUAN	L/L	0	0	7.88	16	12	0	3/16/92	San Pedro de Macoris, D.R.
36	WILL HARRIS	R/R	3	2	2.98	52	7	2	8/28/84	Houston, TX
51	JAMES HOYT	R/R	1	0	4.38	66	14	0	9/30/86	Boise, ID
60	DALLAS KEUCHEL	L/L	14	5	2.90	125	47	0	1/1/88	Tulsa, OK
46	FRANCISCO LIRIANO	L/L	6	7	5.66	85	53	0	10/26/83	San Cristobal, D.R.
58	FRANCIS MARTES	R/R	5	2	5.80	69	31	0	11/24/95	Couti, D.R.
43	LANCE McCULLERS JR.	L/R	7	4	4.25	132	40	0	10/2/93	Tampa, FL
31	COLLIN McHUGH	R/R	5	2	3.55	62	20	0	6/19/87	Naperville, IL
50	CHARLIE MORTON	R/R	14	7	3.62	163	50	0	11/12/83	Flemington, NJ
59	JOE MUSGROVE	R/R	7	8	4.77	98	28	2	12/4/92	El Cajon, CA
41	BRAD PEACOCK	R/R	13	2	3.00	161	57	0	2/2/88	Palm Beach, FL
29	TONY SIPP	L/L	0	1	5.79	39	16	0	7/12/83	Pascagoula, MS
35	JUSTIN VERLANDER	R/R	15	8	3.36	219	72	0	2/20/83	Manakin-Sabot, VA

NO.	PLAYER	B/T	AB	H	AVG	HR	RBI	OBP	BIRTHDATE	BIRTHPLACE
CATCHERS										
30	JUAN CENTENO	L/R	52	12	.231	2	4	.286	11/16/89	Arecibo, Puerto Rico
11	EVAN GATTIS	R/R	300	79	.263	12	55	.311	8/18/86	Dallas, TX
16	BRIAN McCANN	L/R	349	84	.241	18	62	.323	2/20/84	Athens, GA
12	MAX STASSI	R/R	24	4	.167	2	4	.323	3/15/91	Woodland, CA
INFIELDERS										
27	JOSE ALTUVE	R/R	590	204	.346	24	81	.410	5/6/90	Maracay, Venezuela
2	ALEX BREGMAN	R/R	556	158	.284	19	71	.352	3/30/94	Albuquerque, NM
1	CARLOS CORREA	R/R	422	133	.315	24	84	.391	9/22/94	Ponce, Puerto Rico
28	J.D. DAVIS	R/R	62	14	.226	4	7	.279	4/27/93	Elk Grove, CA
10	YULI GURRIEL	R/R	529	158	.299	18	75	.332	6/9/84	Sancti Spiritus, Cuba
38	COLIN MORAN	L/R	11	4	.364	1	3	.417	10/1/92	Port Chester, NY
23	A.J. REED	L/L	6	0	.000	0	0	.000	5/10/93	Terre Haute, IN
13	TYLER WHITE	R/R	61	17	.279	3	10	.328	10/29/90	Mooresboro, NC
OUTFIELDERS										
15	CARLOS BELTRÁN	S/R	467	108	.231	14	51	.283	4/24/77	Manati, Puerto Rico
21	DEREK FISHER	L/R	146	31	.212	5	17	.307	8/21/93	Lebanon, PA
9	MARWIN GONZALEZ	S/R	455	138	.303	23	90	.377	3/14/89	Puerto Ordaz, Venezuela
18	TONY KEMP	L/R	37	8	.216	0	4	.256	10/31/91	Franklin, TN
6	JAKE MARISNICK	R/R	230	56	.243	16	35	.319	3/30/91	Riverside, CA
3	CAMERON MAYBIN	R/R	395	90	.228	10	35	.318	4/4/87	Asheville, NC
22	JOSH REDDICK	L/R	477	150	.314	13	82	.363	2/19/87	Savannah, GA
4	GEORGE SPRINGER	R/R	548	155	.283	34	85	.367	9/19/89	New Britain, CT

Manager: A.J. Hinch (14). **Coaches:** Craig Bjornson (52), Alex Cora (26), Rich Dauer (48), Dave Hudgens (39), Gary Pettis (8), Alonzo Powell (55), Brent Strom (56).

REGULAR-SEASON RESULTS

MONTH-BY-MONTH RECORD

APRIL
16–9

MAY
22–7

JUNE
16–11

JULY
15–9

AUGUST
11–17

SEPTEMBER
20–8

OCTOBER
1–0

2017 RECORD
101–61

THE ASTROS FINISHED THE REGULAR SEASON WITH OVER 100 WINS FOR THE FIRST TIME SINCE 1998, AND ONLY THE SECOND TIME IN FRANCHISE HISTORY.

BY GEORGE

ASTROS SLUGGER GEORGE SPRINGER TALKS
ABOUT HIS TEAM'S STELLAR SEASON AND
COMPETITORS FAR TOUGHER THAN THE
OPPONENTS ON THE FIELD — HIS FAMILY.

BY BRIAN McTAGGART

George Springer, the Astros' high-flying center fielder, has
endeared himself to fans in Houston with his up-tempo style
of play since making his Big League debut in 2014, and this year
he's emerged on the national stage, too. After playing in all 162
games in 2016, Springer was selected to the American League
All-Star team for the first time this year, starting in left field.

As the leadoff hitter for the team that held the best record
in the AL for much of the season (until the Indians won 20-
plus straight games, at least) and won the AL West in runaway
fashion — the Astros' first division title since 2001 — Springer
is the ignition switch for one of the most dangerous lineups in
the game. He possesses a devastating speed/power combination
that boosts his team more than most superstars can.

Life is pretty good away from the field, too, as the
28-year-old Springer has recently gotten engaged to his
long-time girlfriend and tries to live a quiet life away from
the ballpark, which means he stays off social media as much
as possible. When he's at the yard, the smiling, dancing
Springer makes it clear he's having the time of his life in
Houston, a point made crystal clear when we caught up with
him in the final weeks of the season.

*The Astros led the AL West the entire season and had opened up
a big lead by the end of May. How did the team manage to stay
focused on its goals?*
The goal was obviously to win the division, win each series, and
just keep playing hard.

*What kind of impact has a veteran like Carlos Beltran had on you
and some of the other younger players?*
He's been everything, from his experience to his knowledge
to his calm demeanor. He's helped me tremendously, and I
know he's helped all 25-plus guys in here.

The Astros have a young core — you, Carlos Correa, Alex Bregman, Jose Altuve — that could be together for a long time. How exciting is it to be a part of that?
It's an honor, man. It's awesome. It's fun. The talent that's in this room is, I believe, a special group of guys. To have a shot to be part of it, I'm happy.

What was it like making your first All-Star team and having so many teammates with you in Miami in July?
It was awesome. It's a pretty indescribable feeling to be out there playing in a game that I've watched my whole life, especially with five or six of my teammates — three of them starting. That was an unbelievable experience.

Have you felt like you've emerged as a leader in the clubhouse for the Astros, and is that a role you have now come to embrace?
I show up every day and be myself, and if that helps somebody, great. If not, I understand. I just like to be myself.

You have been known to run into walls to make a catch. Are you just as adventurous in your everyday life?
In a controlled environment, yeah. I don't put myself in harm's way, but I like to have fun.

You came from a very athletic family. What was that experience like growing up?
(Springer's father, George Jr., played in the 1976 Little League baseball World Series and played football at UConn; his mother, Laura, was a top-level gymnast; both of his sisters played softball in college.) Constant competition. Every single day there was something between me and my sisters or me and my parents. It was a constant competition in our household.

How did that help you get to where you are now?
You're used to competition every day. You have that fight, you have that desire to go out and beat whoever it is you're competing against, even if at the time it was my sister.

You've said you looked up to Torii Hunter while growing up. Is it daunting to know there are young kids looking up to you?
I actually haven't even thought about that. It is humbling to see kids wearing anybody's jersey. I think that's awesome. It's my job to go out there and set a good example. I'm happy to do so.

You got engaged to your girlfriend, Charlise, and proposed to her on the beach in Cabo San Lucas, Mexico. How has she inspired you?
She's awesome. She's the humbler, the rock. She's there for me when I need her. She's at every game. It's been fun.

As a former softball player, does she analyze your game?
At times I feel she knows the game a little too well because she lets me know if I do anything wrong or whatever the case (laughs). She understands the game and how hard it is to play, but she also knows the stuff a player has to do to play every day, whether it's getting an extra hour of sleep, eating healthier or sitting down on the couch and chilling. She's a very selfless person. She lets me do what I have to do, and I don't really think I can ask for anything more.

We've seen you dancing in the dugout. Where did you get those moves?
Just let your body do what it wants to do. Sometimes you can't contain yourself.

You've been very open about your stutter and started a charity bowling event a few years ago. How gratifying has it been to help so many kids?
It's awesome. It means a lot to me. It's something that's very near and dear to my heart. I'm glad I can help some kids come out of their shell and embrace life.

The Astros led the AL all season long. Have you felt this year that anything short of winning the World Series would be a disappointment?
I think every team's goal every year is to win the World Series. Anything less, yeah, is obviously disappointing.

Brian McTaggart has covered the Astros since 2004, and for MLB.com since 2009.

SPRINGER LED THE 2017 ASTROS WITH 34 HOME RUNS AND WAS SECOND IN THE CLUB WITH 85 RBI IN THE REGULAR SEASON. HE REACHED CAREER HIGHS IN HOME RUNS, RBI, BATTING AVERAGE AND SLUGGING PERCENTAGE.

WORLD SERIES
CHAMPIONS
2017

HOUSTON, WE HAVE LIFTOFF

ROCKETS FLY WHENEVER CARLOS CORREA STEPS TO THE PLATE.

BY BRIAN McTAGGART

At just 23 years old, Astros shortstop Carlos Correa has accomplished more than most of his peers in just three Major League seasons.

Correa, the No. 1 overall pick in the 2012 MLB Draft, made his debut with the Astros in June 2015 at age 20 and promptly won the American League Rookie of the Year Award. In 2016, his first full season in the Big Leagues, he hit .274 with 20 home runs and 96 RBI in 153 games.

After adding veterans like Josh Reddick, Brian McCann and Carlos Beltran before this season, the Astros conquered the Dodgers in the Fall Classic to win the franchise's first title. And at a ripe young age, Correa has already won a World Series title. The Puerto Rico native spoke with us about his formula for success and ambitions for the future.

What did you work the hardest on this spring to put yourself in the best position to succeed this year?
I tried to last 162 games without getting tired, working on my endurance and trying to get faster and stronger. And, obviously, my offense. I want to be a better hitter than I already am, and I feel like I can get so much better. All I did was work on mechanics, work on my approach and work on the things that clicked for me throughout 2015 and '16. I also tried to fix the little things that made me struggle.

You debuted in the Big Leagues at 20 years old. What was the most important thing you learned from being on that stage so young?

Hitting is what you learn the most. Just having a better approach, being more selective in the strike zone — all those types of things that make you a better hitter.

You've already hit more home runs than any other shortstop in Astros history (66 in 361 games). Is it surprising?
Yeah, it's very special. But hopefully I can hit a lot more.

What's it like playing alongside three-time American League batting champion Jose Altuve, who's one of the best hitters in the game?
It's something special. When you see that guy consistently getting two hits a day, it's special to watch. Two-hundred hits for four years in a row, an All-Star, a Silver Slugger, a batting champion, you name it. It's really special to watch him play.

Brian McTaggart has covered the Astros since 2004, and for MLB.com since 2009.

> **"Just having a better approach, being more selective in the strike zone — all those types of things make you a better hitter."**
>
> CARLOS CORREA

CORREA REPRESENTED HIS HOME COUNTRY OF PUERTO RICO IN THE 2017 WORLD BASEBALL CLASSIC. IN A SEMIFINAL GAME AGAINST THE NETHERLANDS, THE YOUNG SHORTSTOP CRUSHED A MOONSHOT TO TIE THE GAME AT 2.

CORREA AND ALTUVE IGNITED THE ASTROS OFFENSE DURING MUCH OF THE 2017 REGULAR SEASON. THE TWO LED THE TEAM IN BATTING AVERAGE, ON-BASE AND SLUGGING PERCENTAGE.

BEST PHOTOS OF 2017

HAIR-RAISING

The Astros did not lack astonishing talent in 2017, and relied on a few mainstays, as well as some newcomers, to post the franchise's second-highest win total ever. Southpaw Dallas Keuchel (top) regained his Cy Young form, posting his third season with an ERA below 3.00. Rookie Yuli Gurriel (opposite), signed as an international free agent last season, led all MLB rookies in batting average. And of course, three-time AL batting champion Jose Altuve anchored the potent Houston attack, slashing .346/.410/.547 in the regular season and coming through in the clutch all postseason long.

CHARGED UP
Carlos Correa (left) and Josh Reddick were both integral parts of a Houston offense that finished first in the Bigs in average and OPS. Reddick hit over .300 for the first time in his career.

JUST IN TIME
The acquisition of Justin Verlander proved to be the biggest move of the summer, as the former AL Cy Young Award winner earned ALCS MVP honors for his stellar outings against the Yankees.

A LEAP FORWARD

The Houston outfield emerged as one of baseball's best, boasting three players with more than 15 home runs in 2017. George Springer (center) was the star of the show, blasting 34 homers and scoring 112 runs while hitting primarily in the leadoff spot in a breakout season.

A WORLD OF FUN

Several of Houston's stars played in the 2017 World Baseball Classic. Tyler Clippard (bottom right) and Alex Bregman (top left) took home the trophy with Team USA.

HOUSTON ASTROS

2017 MINOR LEAGUE RESULTS

AAA FRESNO GRIZZLIES (77-65)

2nd in Pacific Coast League Pacific–North Division

AA CORPUS CHRISTI HOOKS (67-71)

2nd in Texas League South Division

HIGH-A BUIES CREEK ASTROS (74-65)

1st in Carolina League Southern Division

CLASS-A QUAD CITIES RIVER BANDITS (79-59)

1st in Midwest League Western Division

SHORT-SEASON A TRI-CITY VALLEYCATS (34-39)

3rd in New York–Penn League Stedler Division

ROOKIE GREENEVILLE ASTROS (33-34)

2nd in Appalachian League West Division

ROOKIE GCL ASTROS (27-27)

3rd in Gulf Coast League East Division

ZOBRIST LED THE CUBS TO THEIR FIRST WORLD SERIES TITLE IN 108 YEARS, AS CHICAGO OUTLASTED THE INDIANS IN SEVEN GAMES IN ONE OF THE BEST MATCHUPS IN FALL CLASSIC HISTORY.

WORLD SERIES MEMORIES

2016: BIG BEN

Entering the 2016 Fall Classic, the Cubs infamously had not won a title in 108 years, while the Indians' drought approached 68 seasons.

Up and down the Cubs' roster, player after player was worthy of MVP consideration. But as the champagne bottles popped and chants of "Go Cubs Go" resonated throughout Progressive Field after the North Siders won Game 7, it was Ben Zobrist who unassumingly stepped into the spotlight to claim his World Series MVP Award.

Heading into the decisive game, Zobrist owned a .391 average and .462 on-base percentage over 23 World Series at-bats. He boasted nine hits, most notably an RBI triple in Game 2, to help Chicago secure its first win on the road. But with the Series on the line in Game 7, Zobrist saved his best for last, smacking a 10th-inning RBI double to plate the go-ahead run.

The hit brought his slugging percentage for the Series to .500, tying him with Kris Bryant for the second-best mark on the team, behind Anthony Rizzo, and making him the first-ever Cubs player to take home World Series MVP honors.

1967: GOING THE DISTANCE

Three years earlier, in 1964, legendary hurler Bob Gibson came back on two days' rest to start and win an epic World Series Game 7 against the Yankees, as the Cardinals took a 7-5 victory and the world championship. In '67, Gibson would find himself on the hill for another deciding Game 7, this time against a Boston Red Sox lineup that featured Carl Yastrzemski and Jim Lonborg.

All Gibson did was toss his third complete game of the Series, giving up a pair of runs, striking out 10 *and* hitting a home run at the plate in his squad's 7-2 triumph. The victory pushed his World Series winning streak to five games, but perhaps more impressively was just one of Gibson's eight career complete games in the Fall Classic. Only Christy Mathewson and Chief Bender have more.

1997: SANDY'S DANDY

One of the most popular players in Indians history, Sandy Alomar Jr.'s best season came during the Tribe's run to the '97 Series. He finished the regular season with a .324 average and 21 home runs, earned All-Star Game MVP honors, and finished 14th in American League MVP voting.

The Indians may have lost the Series, but not on account of Alomar. In his second World Series with the club, he hit .367 with a pair of homers through the seven games.

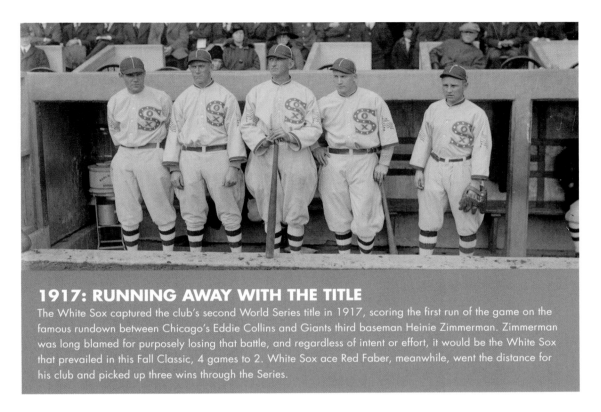

1917: RUNNING AWAY WITH THE TITLE

The White Sox captured the club's second World Series title in 1917, scoring the first run of the game on the famous rundown between Chicago's Eddie Collins and Giants third baseman Heinie Zimmerman. Zimmerman was long blamed for purposely losing that battle, and regardless of intent or effort, it would be the White Sox that prevailed in this Fall Classic, 4 games to 2. White Sox ace Red Faber, meanwhile, went the distance for his club and picked up three wins through the Series.

2007: HIGH AND LOWELL

The 2007 World Series featured a newcomer in the Rockies and one of baseball's most storied franchises in the Red Sox. Boston swept Colorado in four games to earn its second title in four years.

Red Sox veteran Mike Lowell, who placed fifth in AL MVP voting for the 2007 season, became only the second Puerto Rican player (the first being Hall of Famer Roberto Clemente) to garner World Series MVP honors. He batted .400 with three doubles, a home run and four RBI in the four-game set.

He and his teammate, Josh Beckett, who was named Series MVP in the '03 Fall Classic when they were both on the Marlins, became the first duo to each get a World Series MVP nod by winning a title with a team in each league.

1992:
EXPANDING BORDERS

For a brief stretch in the early 1990s, MLB's model franchise was situated in Ontario, Canada. The Blue Jays had a state-of-the-art facility in SkyDome, President and CEO Paul Beeston and General Manager Pat Gillick were highly respected figures in the industry, and Manager Cito Gaston, in his fourth season, had a reputation for giving his players a wide range of freedom.

Toronto would make its mark in the record books in 1992 (one year before Joe Carter's famous walk-off home run), becoming the first franchise outside of the U.S. to win a World Series. Stalwart catcher Pat Borders, previously overshadowed by the likes of John Olerud, Roberto Alomar and Carter, took the spotlight in the Fall Classic. He earned MVP honors, hitting .450 and catching every inning of the Series, including all 11 frames of the clinching Game 6. The championship yielded the first of the franchise's back-to-back trophies.

1947: RISE OF THE ROOKIE

With everyone finally back from the war, the Yankees and Dodgers resumed the rivalry that had begun in 1941. The 1947 World Series featured the debut of the first African-American player to appear in the postseason — Dodgers rookie Jackie Robinson, who had broken the MLB color barrier at the start of the regular season. Robinson went 7 for 27 with three RBI and a pair of stolen bases, but the Blue Crew fell to the Bronx Bombers in seven games.

After a season in which he led the National League in stolen bases (29), Robinson would go on to be named the first-ever Rookie of the Year, an honor renamed the Jackie Robinson Award 40 years later as an homage to its first recipient.

2002: MONKEY BUSINESS

The small-ball Anaheim Angels won the all-California matchup in the franchise's first World Series since its founding in 1961 — and the Halos also showed they could flex their muscles. They had seven home runs in the Fall Classic, including three by Series MVP Troy Glaus, who batted .385 with eight RBI.

The Series went a full seven games after Anaheim was able to come back in Game 6. The notorious Rally Monkey was gyrating on the scoreboard screen, prompting the crowd of 44,506 at Edison Field to go bananas, and the Angels' hitters took the cue, thrilling their fans.

Glaus started the rally with a single, and the rest of the game went like a Disney script. In his next at-bat, he hit the go-ahead double that put the Halos up, 6–5, and forced a Game 7, which the Angels won thanks to a combined six-hitter from their pitching staff.

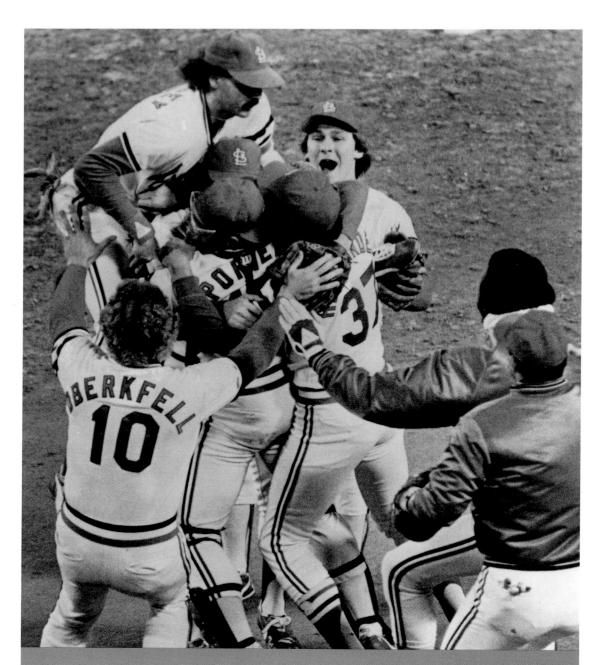

1982: REDBIRDS FLY HIGH

Everything fell into place for the 1982 Milwaukee Brewers, nicknamed "Harvey's Wallbangers," after skipper Harvey Kuenn. Robin Yount led the pennant-winning Brewers, winning a Gold Glove and also pacing the American League in hits, doubles, OPS and total bases. His Milwaukee squad fell to the Cardinals in seven games, though, as St. Louis scored five runs in the final three innings to seal the deal. St. Louis catcher Darrell Porter hit .286 to earn MVP honors in his second World Series appearance.

2005: WILD PUMA

The Astros were able to bring the Fall Classic to Houston for the first time in franchise history in 2005, facing off against the Chicago White Sox but losing in four straight heartbreaking games.

Texas native Lance Berkman, who mashed 24 home runs during the regular season, led the Houston offense with six RBI and a .385/.526/.538 slash line in the Series.

While it may have been the only World Series that Berkman, who spent 11.5 seasons with the Astros, played in for the club, "Big Puma" made his first trip to the Fall Classic count.

1957: BRAVE BURDETTE

While perennial 20-game winner Warren Spahn may have led the Milwaukee Braves to the postseason, it was Lew Burdette who was the dominant presence in the 1957 World Series. He went the distance in Game 2, picking up five strikeouts in a complete-game effort. He was virtually unhittable, as the Braves beat the Yankees in seven games to capture Milwaukee's first championship, becoming the first pitcher since Christy Mathewson to throw two shutouts in a World Series.

Burdette tossed three complete games in a row and dazzled the Yankees with 24 consecutive shutout innings. He outdueled Whitey Ford, 1-0, in Game 5, then returned to pitch the decisive seventh game on two days' rest when Milwaukee's ace, Warren Spahn, came down with the flu. Burdette responded with a 5-0 victory over Don Larsen in the Series clincher.

MAJOR LEAGUE BASEBALL

President, Business & Media	Bob Bowman
Executive Vice President, Content; Editor-in-Chief, MLBAM	Dinn Mann
Vice President, Consumer Media	Donald S. Hintze
Editorial Director	Mike McCormick
Account Executive	Jake Schwartzstein
Specialist, Content Media	Alex Trautwig
Project Art Director	Melanie Finnern
Project Assistant Editor	Joe Sparacio
Editorial Interns	Adriana Belmonte
	Dylan Hornik

MAJOR LEAGUE BASEBALL PHOTOS

Manager	Jessica Carroll
Photo Editor	Jim McKenna

WORLD SERIES CONTRIBUTING PHOTOGRAPHERS

LG Patterson, Alex Trautwig, Rob Tringali

PENGUIN RANDOM HOUSE CANADA TEAM

President & CEO	Brad Martin
President & Publisher	Kristin Cochrane
VP, Publisher, McClelland & Stewart	Jared Bland
SVP, Director of Production	Janine Laporte
Associate Managing Editor	Kimberlee Hesas
Editorial Assistant	Joe Lee
Assistant Manager, Production	Christie Hanson
Executive Sales Director	Scott Loomer
Imprint Sales Director	Bonnie Maitland
Publicity Manager	Ruta Liormonas
Senior Designer	Five Seventeen
Typesetter/Design Associate	Erin Cooper